Textures & Colours
for Interiors

Textures & Colours for Interiors

AN INSPIRATIONAL GUIDE TO DECORATING YOUR HOME

text by Katherine Sorrell

APPLE

Credits

Senior project editor   Nicolette Linton
Senior art editor   Penny Cobb
Designer   Justina Leitão
Cover design   Anne Burdick
Text editors   Morag Lyall, Pat Farrington
Picture Research   Darren Wisdom@Image Select
   International, Laurent Boubounelle
Swatch Photographer   Martin Norris
Illustrator   Jane Smith
Indexer   Pamela Ellis

Art director   Moira Clinch
Publisher   Piers Spence

Manufactured by Regent Publishing Services Ltd,
   Hong Kong
Printed by Winner Printing and Packing Ltd, China

Quarto would like to thank and acknowledge Annette Main
and Frances Eustace for sourcing the swatches for the book.

Quarto would also like to thank and acknowledge the
following for supplying pictures reproduced in this book.

(Key: l left, r right, c centre, t top, b bottom)

Asplund: p85t; G.P.& J. Baker: p55; Cassina: p36/Photo:
Andrea Ferrari; The Conran Shop: p19; p24b; p30r; p35r;
p59l; p60; p64; p77; Andreas Von Einsiedel: p102; Fired
Earth: p2; p10; p40t; p44t&b; p48r; p82; p106t&b; Good
Housekeeping Syndication: p73l; Habitat: p35l; p47b; p65r;
p76t; p83; p111r; Harvey Jones: p33t; p69; p101; The
Holding Company/Camron Public Relations Ltd.: p31; p36r;
p42r; p45r; p47l; p49b; p61b; IKEA: p67r; IKEA/Condor
P.R. Ltd.: p72l&r; p76b; p78; p79l; p96t; p100r; p108;
p109l&r; p111c; The Interior Archive: p8- Bob Smith/Artist:
Johny Woodford; p16- Herbert Ypma/Designer: Deamer
Phillips; p17- Henry Wilson/Designer: Colin Duckworth;
p20t- Henry Wilson/Designer: Chris Davies; p21- Henry
Wilson/Designer: Colin Duckworth; p22- D. von
Schaewen/Maison Française; p23r- Ken Hayden/Designer:
Jonathan Reed; p27b- Simon Brown/Designer: Margaret
Howell; p39b- Bob Smith/Owner: Ricardo; p46- Edina van
der Wyck/Designer: Atlanta Bartlett; page 49t- Andrew
Wood; p52- Ken Hayden/Owner: Sue Flegg; p53- Ken
Hayden/Property: Cromwell Tower; p57t- Bob
Smith/Owner: Lassman; p58- Henry Wilson; p68r Simon
Brown/Designer: Margaret Howell; p74b- Simon Brown;
p84- Nadia Mackenzie/Designer: Lisa Guild; p90-Nadia
Mackenzie/Designer: Lisa Guild; p92t- Nadia
Mackenzie/Florist: Paula Pryke, b Henry Wilson/Designer:
Antonio; p100l- Henry Wilson; Inside Stock Image
Production/The Interior Archive: p20b- House &
Leisure/Ryno; p29- House & Leisure/Ryno; p37- House &
Leisure/Ryno; p41- House & Leisure/J. de Villiers; p43-
House & Leisure/Ryno; p62- House & Leisure; p66- House
& Leisure/M. Hoyle; p85b- House & Leisure/J. de Villiers;
p87l- Maison Française/C. Sarramon; p91t- House &
Leisure/P. Baasch; p104; IPC Syndication: p9- Tom
Leighton/Homes & Gardens; p18t- Winifred Heinze/Homes
& Gardens; p23l- Tom Stewart/Homes & Gardens; p24t
Polly Wreford/Homes & Gardens; p25l- Simon
Whitmore/Ideal Home, r Polly Wreford/Homes & Gardens;
p40b- Tim Young/Homes & Gardens; p42l- Mark
Williams/Homes & Gardens; p54- John Mason/ Homes &
Gardens; p56- Polly Wreford/Homes & Gardens; p57b-
Simon Whitmore/ Ideal Home; p63t- Alex Ramsay/Homes &
Gardens; p65l- Peter Aprahamian/Living Etc.; p67l- Winfried
Heinze/ Homes & Gardens; p70- Kim Sayer/Homes &
Gardens; p71- Gary Hammill/Ideal Home; p74t- Caroline
Arber/Homes & Gardens; p91b- Pia Trude/Homes &
Gardens; p93- Tim Young/Living Etc.; p94- Tom
Leighton/Homes & Gardens; p97- Simon Whitmore/Ideal
Home; p98- Kim Sayer/Homes & Gardens; p105b- Nick
Pope/Living Etc; p107- Alex Ramsay/Homes & Gardens;
Kudos Features Ltd./Brian Harrison: p26; p89t ; ligne roset:
p6; p7; p11; p12; p88br; p99t; The Linwood Fabric
Company: p86; Malabar Cotton Company: p88bl; p95r;
Marks & Spencer: p18b; p27t; p39t; p48l; p59r; p63b; p68l;
p73r; p87r; p95l; p96b; p99b; p103; p105t; p111l;Monkwell
Collection:p28t&b; p30l; p61t;Pictures Colour Library:p38;
p45l; p110; Purves & Purves: p79r; p89br;Smallbone: p32;
p33b; p34; p75

All other photographs and illustrations are the copyright of
Quarto Publishing plc. While every effort has been made to
credit contributors, Quarto would like to apologise should
there have been any omissions or errors.

Imprint

First published in the United Kingdom
by the Apple Press
6 Blundell Street
London N7 9BH

ISBN 1-84092-309-1

A QUARTO BOOK

This book was designed and produced by
Quarto Publishing plc
The Old Brewery
6 Blundell Street
London N7 9BH

10 9 8 7 6 5 4 3 2 1

AUTHOR'S ACKNOWLEDGMENTS

Katherine Sorrell would like to thank her
nily, friends and colleagues for their constant and
ng support, advice and help. She would also like
to thank the following people and organisations:

chen Specialists' Association; Andrew Barr at the
chen Clinic; Spencer Swaffer at Spencer Swaffer
ques; The Brick Development Association; Suna
Pollard; World's End Tiles; Totem Design.

Contents

INTRODUCTION   6

NEUTRALS   14-49
Introduction   16
Living   18
Sleeping   26
Eating   32
Bathing   40
Working and playing   46

SOFT COLOURS   50-79
Introduction   52
Living   54
Sleeping   60
Eating   66
Bathing   72
Working and playing   76

STRONG COLOURS   80-111
Introduction   82
Living   84
Sleeping   90
Eating   98
Bathing   104
Working and playing   108

PRACTICAL
INFORMATION   112

INDEX   122

INTRODUCTION

Have you ever walked into a room and felt instantly at home? Or, conversely, inexplicably ill at ease? Such feelings arise from a combination of factors: the room's size and proportions, its light (both natural and artificial), the shapes, styles and layout of the furniture, colours and patterns used and, perhaps more subliminally, the mix of textures.

To consider texture as important an element of interior design as, say, colour or the arrangement of furnishings, is a way of thinking that's both ancient and highly contemporary. Human beings have always had a basic need for warmth, privacy, a safe haven to which we can retreat; and to create a home that satisfies those needs is about much more than putting together a few rooms that look good. To be satisfying on all levels – not just aesthetically, but also physically and emotionally – a home needs to feel

right. And in today's fast-paced, stressed-out world, it couldn't be more important that your home is a cocooning, comfortable and relaxing place in which to refresh your spirits and recharge your energies in readiness for the demands of modern life.

Rediscover your sense of touch

So how does texture contribute to all this? On a practical level, using the right material in the right area can be a purely functional choice, from a non-slip bathroom floor to a soft and cozy throw on a bed. On a more spiritual level, however, an enjoyment of all that texture has to offer satisfies our often forgotten sense of touch, our primal need to relate to our surroundings in a direct and basic way. An understanding of this need has become evident in recent decorating trends, which have tended toward purity and clean lines, lack of clutter and an holistic appreciation of our homes (such as the Eastern art of *feng shui*). 'Texture is the new colour' may be a snappy phrase, but it's best, however, not to think of using texture as following a particular fashion, but to use it as a means of living in a way that's

🔺 This witty, quirky vase is attractive and unusual, and provides stunning textural intrigue.

◀ A combination of smooth, sleek leather with a variety of rough, three-dimensional surfaces demonstrates just how powerful the impact of texture can be.

▼ Mix strong colours and characterful
textures for a look that has vigour and verve.

pleasurable and nurturing, thoughtful and sophisticated, practical and intuitive.

To get the best from textures in the home it's a good idea to gain a little understanding of the different types of texture and how they work, both individually and together. The basic starting point is usually hard and soft but, just as there's more to colour than primaries and secondaries, there are numerous ways of considering texture, with infinite subtle variations and satisfying combinations. Between hard and soft, for example, there's a sort of 'giving' hardness, as found in wood, coir or vinyl. As well as matt and glossy, there are dull sheens and satiny finishes; there's rough and smooth, which is closely related to, but not the same as, hairy and silky; there's warm and cool, heavy and light, clear and opaque, dimpled, ridged, creased, frosted, riven, knobbly, sheer: the list is restricted only by your ability to observe what's around you and to stretch your imagination.

Creating a textural room

In general, hard textures provide the backbone of a room and soft textures a gentler counterpoint. Harder textures are often (but not always) quite smooth and shiny, soft ones rougher and more matt. So, without trying very hard, it's easy to achieve a basic textural structure. An interesting, enjoyable mix of textures can result from the use of just two wildly contrasting materials, or from dozens of subtly different ones. A good balance is important, though it's not a question of matching equal amounts of one texture with its opposite – that may, in fact, only result in them detracting from each other. Play around and be open-minded, remembering that texture doesn't just work on its own but has a big influence on all the other essentials of decorating; mixing hard and soft textures prevents a room from having either a tinny echo or sounding too 'dead', while three-dimensional textures are needed as a counterpoint to smooth,

◐ Laid-back, neutral schemes often show textures at their best. In this smart dining area the colours used are superbly subtle and the textures full of interest.

flat ones in order to provide visual interest. And very shiny, glossy textures throw light back into a room, while matt ones absorb it.

Think of layering one texture with another, then perhaps adding touches of one or two more. The aim is to achieve contrasts rather than clashes, so it may be best not to pick the more extreme, unusual textures until you feel confident in using them; certainly it's inadvisable to use too many whimsical textures in one space – unless you're aiming for that eccentric look. Don't be too timid, though; rooms composed all of similar textures have no life and will be just as unpleasant to live in as those that are overly stimulating.

What about colour, you may wonder? The relationship between colour and texture is an interesting one, and the two are often hard to separate. The same colour can appear subtly (or even strikingly) different when applied to two different textures, and sometimes it's hard to know which of the two qualities is making more of an impact. Using plain colours, or at least very understated patterns, rather than complex, decorative designs, does, however, undoubtedly enhance textural effect: who needs busy prints when you can have the glorious grain of wood, the linear weave of bouclé sisal, unevenly pitted limestone, fluffy tufts of mohair or the waffles of an old-fashioned blanket? Keep colours simple and you almost can't go wrong.

When planning your textural themes, consider the room's size and proportions first. Do you want to bring out the cosiness of a small bedroom, for example, with a flokati

A shiny chrome shower head makes a wonderful impression when offset by the matt patina of mosaic tiles.

rug on top of a luxurious carpet, matt-painted walls, velvet drapes and mohair throws? Or would it be nice to emphasise the light and airy nature of a living room with satin-varnished floorboards, glossy woodwork, sheer drapes and shot silk cushions? Think, too, about architectural features. A Georgian house with intricate cornicing and sash windows, for example, may not benefit from over-the-top use of cowhide, galvanised steel or grooved rubber, but needs a more subtle approach, using classic materials such as wood, stone and glass. In a Modernist flat, on the other hand, where concrete, glass and steel will probably already dominate, you may wish to use a range of more forgiving textures that will add comfort without detracting from the nature of the building itself.

Structural starting points

When designing a room, one texture is likely to dominate, and it's often that of the floor – usually the largest clear area in the room, and one that can be as understated or as visually striking as you wish. Walls, too, play an enormous part, and while they can be simply painted with matt emulsion to provide a neutral backdrop for everything else, there is always the option of making them texturally interesting in their own right. These two elements, then, are likely to be your starting point, and it's really worth spending the time and effort (but not necessarily money) on getting them right before you rush into buying furniture and accessories. It's best, for example, to avoid really overpowering textures, instead, choose something that's subtle but still interesting. Points of eye-catching interest can always be created in the form of a rug, wall panel or painting.

Other structural elements – kitchen work surfaces and cupboard doors, for example, or sanitary ware in a bathroom – make a big contribution to a room's textural feel. While practicality is likely to be uppermost in your mind, don't overlook the importance of texture when selecting these fittings. If you have large expanses of laminates in a kitchen you might want to add a wired-glass splashback to offset them, while adding a mosaic shower surround could create the ideal contrast to a plain white bathroom suite.

The chances are, though, that where you'll really get to play around with texture is with your choice of furniture, fabrics and accessories. Here you can combine and contrast different surfaces to their utmost potential. The possibilities are endless, from a timeless mix of wood, metal and stone to a groovy choice of rubber, plastic and pashmina; if you bear in mind all the principles outlined above, you can achieve a look that's not just good

▲ In a room that is predominantly hard and smooth, a soft wool rug and woven wicker chair create appealing counterpoints.

but really superb. Even with nothing other than the careful positioning of a few attractive accessories, you can add wonderful textural highlights to a room that will enhance it immeasurably.

Making light work

The final thought when it comes to planning is lighting – though really it should be your first consideration, as impressive, inventive lighting schemes generally need to be installed before walls are plastered and furniture positioned. Good lighting is not only necessary for a room's function and feel, it will also show off its textures to the fullest. Poor lighting, on the other hand, will flatten texture and make the room seem bland and boring. Try to achieve a compromise between the gloomy dimness of under-lighting and the lamp-shop effect of over-lighting by using a variety of overhead, wall, floor and table lamps, some of which could have dimmer switches to give you additional flexibility.

There's no shortage of inspiration to help you plan a textural scheme. Buy or borrow

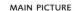 This bedroom balances large expanses of hard and soft textures – the result is both sophisticated and comfortable.

books and magazines, ask for swatches of fabric from shops, keep an eye on fashions in clothing (they'll hit the home a few months later) and generally look closely at what's around, from nature to architecture, people to animals, art galleries to food. Then try to translate what most takes your fancy into your own home. This book will hopefully be an invaluable guide with its photographs, explanations of textural schemes, and swatch files. And the separate Swatch Book can be used to mix and match different textures and help you develop your own ideas.

How to use this book

THIS BOOK IS DIVIDED INTO THREE SECTIONS: NEUTRALS, SOFT COLOURS
AND STRONG COLOURS, EACH OF WHICH CONTAINS CHAPTERS ON ALL THE ESSENTIAL
INTERIOR SPACES: LIVING ROOMS, BEDROOMS, KITCHENS, BATHROOMS,
HOME OFFICES AND PLAYROOMS.

MAIN PICTURE

A beautiful large picture demonstrates ideas and themes for you to emulate.

MAIN TEXT

This explains the thinking behind each textural scheme and outlines alternative ways of creating a similar effect.

SWATCH FILE

These swatches detail the textural elements used in, and inspired by, the schemes shown on each page. The number of each chart relates to the swatch number in the accompanying Swatch Book.

DETAILS

Every main picture is backed up by one or more close-up shots which further explain the look.

Neutral

THE **PLEASURE** OF TEXTURE IS ENHANCED BY THE SUBTLE QUALITIES OF **NATURAL** MATERIALS COMBINED WITH NEUTRAL COLOURS. THIS IS A LOOK THAT **TRULY** WORKS ANYWHERE AND WITH ANY **STYLE**.

colours

NEUTRAL COLOURS

Using a palette of neutral colours is the most obvious starting point for a textural scheme, as the less obvious the colours, the greater the impact of the textures. That's not to say that a neutral scheme need be bland or lacking in vitality: there are endless combinations of neutral colours that have a beauty and character all of their own.

The spectrum of neutrals ranges from black, through grey, to white, as well as cream to chocolate brown via sand, taupe, ivory and ochre. To my mind, you can also include navy blue and metallics: silver and iron in particular, and, to a lesser extent, copper, bronze and gold.

Key materials for such a colour scheme are, understandably, natural ones. Choose bare wood; fibre floorings; wicker, raffia, and rattan; clear glass; stone, undyed skins and fur; brick; terracotta and quarry tiles; and metals. Use with paint colours from the neutral range, and simple fabrics such as unbleached linen, pure white cotton, or tweed in the greys and browns of the Scottish Highlands.

A neutral, natural scheme may be clean and calm, but that doesn't mean it has to be off-putting or uncomfortable. A pale room based around off-whites could, for example, feature suede-covered furniture, cashmere cushions, a fluffy flokati rug, soft woolen throws and delicate muslin drapes, while a more masculine room in greys and black might include furniture in leather or burr walnut, sumptuous velvet drapes, oak floorboards and chrome accessories.

Neutral colours are highly versatile and can be easily adapted, not just for any room in the house, but also for any environment: a country cottage, a city apartment, a seaside retreat. Take pleasure in the infinite variety of effects you can achieve: from the sensuous to the dramatic, the rugged to the urbane. If you wish, include a dash of pastel or bold colour as a contrast or a concession to fashion, but don't forget that the beauty of a neutral scheme is in its laid-back feel, minimal approach, and subtle sophistication.

◖ In a classic sitting room, neutral colours go hand in hand with an attractive range of natural textures.

◖ This light, open kitchen uses a small range of pale, neutral colours for a contemporary feel.

▶ The restrained colours of this inviting room emphasize its intriguing use of boldly contrasting textures, from floor to windows to furniture.

● Lights with strong shapes can be a feature in themselves.

swatch

urban luxury

Choose natural materials for their inherent beauty. Their luxurious textures will help you create a look that's effortlessly chic and simple.

Living room textures

METALLIC PAINT
Metallic paint can be sprayed onto vases, bowls and other accessories for an interesting, inexpensive contrast.
95

TEXTURED SHEER
Sheer fabrics don't need to be plain and boring. This example has a raffia weave for a fabulous three-dimensional texture.
150

SMOOTH LINEN
Plain linen is unobtrusive but has a sophisticated look and feel, whether used for upholstery, cushions or drapes.
179

NATURAL LEATHER
A leather couch like the one shown here has a warm, soft and luxurious surface. It will wear to an attractive patina as it ages.
226

WOOL CARPET
In an understated colour, a tufted carpet or rug can add a delightful bouclé texture that's lovely both to look at and walk on.
259

WOODEN BOARDS
Floorboards can vary greatly in texture. This American white ash is sleek and smooth.
492

Urban luxury

THE SIMPLICITY OF A LIVING ROOM DESIGNED AROUND NEUTRAL COLOURS PROVIDES WELCOME RELIEF FROM HECTIC CITY LIFE WITH CAREFUL PLANNING, THIS TYPE OF SCHEME PROVIDES A RETREAT IN WHICH TO RELAX, RE-ENERGISE AND REFRESH YOUR SPIRITS

Here, leather and velvet are relaxed rather than imposing and the burnished silver vase echoes the metallic legs of the unusual leather coffee table.

Choose luxurious fabrics and plumply padded upholstery and you won't be able to resist throwing yourself onto the couch and putting your feet up. Pale colours – such as sand, taupe, fawn and ivory – can be mixed with darker accents, or you could opt for a bolder look that makes the most of black, navy or chocolate.

Piles of rugs

A beautiful rug can be the focus of a room just as much as a fireplace or a work of art, with the added benefit of providing softness underfoot. And, while colour and pattern are important, texture is crucial: the pile may be short and dense, long and fluffy or, as in the room on the left, cut three-dimensionally for interest and impact. Rugs are enormously versatile (use several different types together in a room for an even more characterful look), and they work particularly well as a foil to wood or stone flooring, though they're just as nice laid over a plain fitted carpet.

The fabrics you select for a living room are all-important. The gentle sheen of leather can be contrasted with the matt depth of velvet, for example, or coarse wool with the silky tactility of chenille. Window treatments benefit from generosity: full-length linen drapes alongside sheer muslin play on the themes of heavy and light, sheer and opaque, while being highly practical, too. Some modern sheer fabrics have fabulous metallic surfaces, crinkle weaves or even patterns made from opaque appliqués – their textural uses are endless.

To create character, use furniture and accessories that have strong shapes – perhaps round, square or rectangular – and add dramatic lighting which will further define their forms and surface finishes.

▲ Mix rough matting, old wood, soft wool blankets and glazed ceramics for textures with an embracing quality.

Country comfort

NATURAL MATERIALS OFFER A VARIETY OF SURFACES THAT ARE
IRRESISTIBLY TACTILE. IF THEY'RE ROUGH, RUGGED OR UNFINISHED
IN APPEARANCE, IT WILL ONLY INCREASE THEIR RUSTIC CHARM.

◀ Somewhere between minimal and ethnic, traditional and modern, this room has a pleasant atmosphere that's neither too grand nor too eclectic.

It's hard to beat the pleasant informality of piles of fat cushions topping a traditional-style couch. To unify this look, ensure that colours are complementary rather than disparate, and that patterns are muted rather than obvious.

The appeal of craft work

The roughness of a woven fibre flooring and the strong lines of wooden furniture provide an attractive background to the room shown opposite – you need hard surfaces to create a structural background, even in a soft and comfortable living area. And in a room like this, it's ideal to display pieces that have a craft-like ethos, an attractive, unsophisticated quality such as country-style stools, vases, lanterns and wood-framed pictures.

Introducing a touch of bold colour or pattern – in the form of a rug, a throw, a painting or a piece of pottery – can enliven a neutral colour scheme without detracting from its subtle sophistication. Earthy or spicy tones are often best, as the geometrically patterned kelim on the left shows. Its woven finish contrasts nicely with the more nubby surface of the coir flooring, which in turn makes a welcome change from walls that have been painted with smooth emulsion.

Think carefully about providing a well-balanced mix of textures – this room, though very simple in style, is full of interesting texture, from the satiny gleam of cast iron and glazed pottery to the roughness of wicker and old wood, to the rather more elegant appearance of a waffle blanket and fake-fur cushion. It just goes to show how deceptive neutral colour schemes can be: the effect here is warm and welcoming in an intriguing yet beguiling way.

country comfort

To create a charming, rural-style room, pick textures that are unsophisticated and unpretentious. Surfaces that are noticeably three-dimensional are important, from thick, soft wool to woven paper, rough plaster to grass-like flooring.

Living room textures

PAPER FLOORING
The straightforward weave of this tough paper flooring is wonderfully textural and would be a pleasure to walk on in bare feet.
297

ROUGH PLASTER
A pitted-plaster wall can make quite an impact – it's a good choice for a living room in which you want to convey a very rustic look.
481

NATURAL FIBRE FLOORING
A natural fleck and chunky weave make this abaca flooring superbly tactile. Its informality would work well in a country-style scheme.
295

BOBBLY FABRIC
Cushions or throws that feature bobbles, fringes or other quirky touches bring dynamism to a country living-room.
121

HEMP WALLPAPER
Instead of conventional wallpaper, woven hemp attached to a paper backing makes a fabulous wallcovering.
309

WOVEN WOOL
Loosely woven wool has the right appearance, providing both visual interest and a sense of understated comfort.
126

◀ Woven baskets come in all shapes and sizes, as well as a vast range of attractive natural colours. They're invaluable as casual storage, and make an easy way to add textural contrast to any room.

Cool character

USING PALE COLOURS EMPHASISES SPACE AND A CLUTTER-FREE ROOM CAN BE LIKE A HOLIDAY HOME IN ITS FEELING OF FREEDOM AND RELAXATION. THAT SAID, AN INTERESTING COMBINATION OF MATERIALS CAN STILL BE INTRIGUING, EVEN FUN.

Panelling walls with wood is one way to add warmth, character and an inherent beauty to a room; contrasted with them in the living room on the far left is the smooth coldness of a stone slab floor and the ridged surface of the bamboo mat – an unusual item that's slightly playful in feel yet at the same time extremely practical. A fluffy flokati rug or a cord carpet would have very different, yet equally attractive, effects. Smoothness is repeated in the fabric that's been used to cover the modular couch: if pale-coloured upholstery appeals to you, ensure the covers can be unzipped and washed by machine.

Fabulous floors

One option if you have wooden boards is to cover them with glossy paint. The ultra-reflective gleam of the floor in the central room shows off to best advantage the timeless yet ever-so-simple combination of wood, cane and metal.

Good-quality wooden floors, however, are best left bare. Parquet is always impressive, and the example on the near left looks good teamed with a darker wood side table. Classic meets contemporary in the choice of a boxy armchair covered in brushed cotton and topped with velvet cushions, while the hide rug pulls the room together with a defiantly individual attitude. Neutral schemes often benefit from just such a dash of personality, whether it's a striped zebrano-wood side table, a hairy throw or an inflatable plastic fruit bowl. It's a basic rule of decorating: plan carefully, but don't be afraid to be yourself.

● An all-white room needn't be devoid of interest: matt walls can be contrasted with a shiny floor, while the natural patina of oak and rattan adds another dimension.

● Animal skins can sometimes come across as rather rustic and unsophisticated; this one, however, is teamed with simple but high-quality materials for a chic, attractive effect.

◐ If this look is simply too neutral for you, don't forget that it would be easy to substitute the rug, pictures or cushions for versions with more dramatic contrasts of texture or colour. Or, perhaps, add some free-standing lamps, place a wicker log basket by the fire or stand some ceramics or candles on the coffee table.

ol character

A plain stone floor is the starting point for a mix of exotic woods and unusual fabrics – an effective way to make a subtle statement in a spacious living area.

Living room textures

1 **GLOSSY PAINT**
The ultra-shiny surface of white floor paint reflects the light for a clean, airy look.

232 **ANIMAL PRINT**
A leopard skin print adds vitality and character – only use it in small doses, though.

511 **EBONY VENEER**
Excellent with pale stone, metal, matt paint and natural fabrics.

168 **WOVEN COTTON**
Heavy cotton is hard-wearing and very easy to care for. Give it a pleasant twist with a textured weave like this.

507 **BAMBOO BOARDS**
Bamboo is a fabulous flooring material: tough, durable, and very good looking.

525 **LIMESTONE SLAB**
Though pricey, stone floors last a lifetime and add plenty of character.

swatch

FOR A LIVING ROOM THAT ENVELOPS YOU
WITH A WELCOMING CALM, CHOOSE A
COLOUR PALETTE THAT RANGES FROM IVORY
TO DARK CHOCOLATE, AND COMBINE WITH
RICH, SOFT, THREE-DIMENSIONAL TEXTURES.

Warm and cosy

▲ While the wooden chest and metal-topped table give this room a hard structure,
the overriding feeling is of luxurious softness, thanks to the stonewashed rug, the
comfortably creased corduroy couch and the knitted cushion covers.

Whether your home is old or new, urban or rural, creating an atmosphere of relaxed indulgence is simply a matter of getting the basics right. A floor in an understated colour – perhaps warm sand, dove grey or pale coffee – is both practical and attractive; choose ribbed wool or sisal for textural interest topped with a rug in similarly simple shades.

Walls can be painted with emulsion for an easy, informal look, or else covered with a textured paper: try hessian, cork, metallic foil or raffia for a more unusual effect. At the windows, maximise light by hanging sheer white muslin from a simple wooden or metal pole – its soft gauziness is yet another interesting texture.

A laid-back look

These are your starting points. Next, consider furniture. You will undoubtedly want a squashy couch with washable loose covers made from a comfy fabric such as brushed cotton, velvet or jumbo cord. An armchair might be in leather or rattan (avoid matching suites if you're aiming for a modern yet laid-back look) with a good reading lamp nearby. Suede or leather cubes in different sizes are sophisticated and versatile, while a square coffee table, in wood, glass or metal, adds a welcome note of hard texture to the mix.

Last, top your seating with a variety of interesting throws and cushions; stick to your basic colour scheme but use your imagination when it comes to choosing fabric: knitted wool, woven leather, linen trimmed with feathers, fleece, denim or silk, for example. And add a few beautiful accessories such as wooden bowls, leather boxes, glass or gourd vases, paper lamps and, of course, some deliciously scented candles.

◗ Cubes covered in sensual suede or soft leather are a modern alternative to the traditional footstool.

◗ A sheer drape contrasts beautifully with the heavier weight of the knitted throws and tufted cushions on the couch. These, in turn, offset the plain walls, textured floor and rattan side chair.

warm and cosy

From floors to furniture, surround yourself with textures that are soft and giving for a sensual effect that's utterly embracing.

Living room textures

WOVEN LEATHER
An exciting, modern look for cushions, this is an attractive alternative to the usual smooth surface of leather.

225

GOATSKIN
Fluffy and comforting, a natural animal skin is incredibly tactile underfoot, though you may prefer a man-made alternative.

236

CORK VENEER
Instead of wallpaper or paint, line one wall of a living room with a thin layer of warm and visually interesting cork.

306

METALLIC PAPER
Thin, crumpled hand-made paper can also be used to cover walls – or to make inset panels – which have instant textural impact.

314

◗ Soft, flickering light and delicate scent: a profusion of candles always makes a welcome addition to a room.

▼ Careful consideration has made this room simple but not bland. The surface of the bedside table, for example, reiterates that of the seagrass flooring, while the planked walls echo the shuttered window.

classic elegance

Classic materials are the hallmark of a smart yet comfortable bedroom such as this. Grainy wood, soft wool and crisp linen all have beautiful understated textures and are timelessly attractive.

Bedroom textures

509   POLISHED WALNUT
Dark and elegant, this wood has a distinctive style that creates subtle impact.

186   COOL LINEN
Linen sheets feel fabulous next to the skin – as anyone who's slept in them will tell you.

282   SISAL CARPET
It's hard on the feet at first, but it doesn't take long to adapt to sisal.

WOOL CARPET
The small bobbles of this carpet give it a lively and interesting texture within a neutral colour scheme.
258

LINEN/COTTON WEAVE
This woven check is sophisticated and simple, with a delightful surface texture.
176

SOFT BLANKET
Choose a double-thickness wool blanket for extra-special warmth and comfort.
241

▲ A jute rug such as this is wonderfully soft. The graphic black edging is a sophisticated touch.

The clean lines of a classically styled bedroom make for the ultimate in rest and relaxation – no mess, no distractions, just a beautiful walnut sleigh bed and invitingly crisp cotton sheets. The trick, of course, is in making it look so easy.

Stylishly understated

A natural fibre floorcovering, for example, comes as a slight surprise in a bedroom, where cozier carpet is the norm. But whether you use seagrass, sisal or jute (the softest underfoot), its ridged weave gives interesting textural contrast and provides a wonderful base for a bed made of polished wood. Of course, if you wished you could always place a small, soft rug beside the bed. Panelling walls up to picture-rail height promotes a snug, enclosed feeling; here, though, matt-painted planks of different widths are a quirky touch.

Textiles take on huge importance in a bedroom, and white cotton or linen sheets and pillowcases are the obvious choice for a pared-down, minimal look. Thoughtful details such as piping, edging or buttons will make all the difference between boring and beautiful (add them yourself to plain, inexpensive bed linen). And layers of warm blankets, especially in winter, are a necessary luxury. You could choose white on white with an old-fashioned waffle texture, or go for the more rustic charm of thick wool that's been stitched or fringed around the edges – each has a rougher, three-dimensional feel that's a natural complement to a scheme such as this.

◀ Generously sized blankets – and lots of them – add a feeling of warmth, comfort and indulgence.

Classic elegance

DESIGNING A BEDROOM THAT'S COMFORTABLE, ATTRACTIVE AND FUNCTIONAL IS MOSTLY A MATTER OF GETTING THE BASICS RIGHT. USE SIMPLE YET HIGH-QUALITY INGREDIENTS FOR A TRADITIONAL LOOK WITH A MODERN TWIST.

Free and easy

RELAX THE RULES AND LET YOUR
PERSONALITY SHINE THROUGH. BEDROOMS
DON'T HAVE TO BE FORMAL, BUT CAN BE FUN
AND FRIENDLY – EVEN A LITTLE BIT FUNKY.

One of the advantages of decorating with neutral colours is that they give you the freedom to experiment within a ready-made structure, so it's easy to create a look that's both coherent and eye-catching. If you want to avoid convention without going overboard on eccentricity, think laterally: the traditional components of a bedroom can often be viewed from a different angle.

Light and bright

For a refreshingly airy look, you could limewash floorboards, allowing the grain to show through, and seal them with a glossy varnish to reflect the light. Paint walls an understated soft, matt white, but add a huge head board (the one on the right was made from an old door) covered in a tactile fabric – think suede, chenille, velvet or jumbo corduroy. One-colour bed linen can be livened up with a witty fake fur throw, a mohair blanket or cushions made from a variety of fabrics and strewn across the bed.

Choose bedroom furniture for its appealing character: perhaps modern and sculptural or '50s style and a little worn-in. Upholstery could be stretch sports fabric, denim, brushed cotton or silk. Then consider accessories: you could contrast a plain, hard floor with a gilt-edged mirror that has crimped edges, put a basket beside the bed to hold magazines, or pile chopped logs into a fireplace. And if you have beautiful shawls, bags or dresses, you may want to hang them around the room, providing accents of colour and texture as well as a welcome expression of your character.

▲ A beaten-up chair found in a junk shop sits happily alongside an oversized mirror – fabrics in neutral colours but subtly different textures hold this look together.

▶ A large bedroom can be made even more comfortable by adding floor cushions on which to read, doze or watch TV.

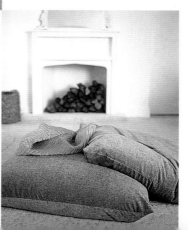

free and easy

Unusual or three-dimensional textures really help add character to a room. And they will always work well together in a neutral colour scheme.

Bedroom textures

TUFTED WOOL
An intriguing fabric such as this would be ideal as an original cushion cover.

122

FLUFFY LAMBSKIN
This Mongolian lambskin has a natural wave and could be used for funky cushions or as a bedside rug.

239

CORD CARPET
This type of carpet is extremely hard-wearing yet very attractive, with a lovely ribbed texture.

274

SYCAMORE FLOORING
Its creamy-gold colour and delicate patterning makes this timber a beautiful choice for a bedroom.

504

FAKE SNAKESKIN
This is a fashionable and unusual fabric that would create instant personality even in an otherwise quite plain room.

222

TEXTURED FABRIC
An unusual weave with raffia-like lumps, this fabric could be used for wall panels or as an impressive bed throw.

307

▶ Curving shapes and soft fabrics emphasize the art of relaxation. Combining a suede-effect head board with a fake fur throw could be over the top – but here the down-to-earth nature of simple cotton sheets and bare floorboards tempers the effect.

Soft sensuality

BEDROOMS BENEFIT FROM A FEELING OF CALM AND TRANQUILLITY
WELL-PLANNED STORAGE MAKES A GOOD START, AND THERE'S ON
OTHER ESSENTIAL – FABRICS THAT IMPLY SINKABLY SOFT COMFORT
WRAPAROUND LUXURY AND NO-HOLDS-BARRED PAMPERING

▲ A pile of cushions can have two purposes: for lounging on and as a still-life arrangement that's as good as any piece of sculpture. Here, three very different textures have been placed together to fabulous effect.

▶ The jumbo cord that surrounds this bed is incredibly appealing. Its linear pattern has been echoed in the knitted throw and the rungs of the wooden ladder.

Combine an open hanging rack with plenty of storage boxes, and you have a bedroom storage system that's highly flexible and relatively inexpensive. This look works best in a modern room – and may need a little effort to keep tidy.

The bed frame is frequently the most dominant feature in a bedroom, so it's often helpful to design the whole scheme around it. You might have an antique sleigh bed made of gorgeous grained wood, or a four-poster with slim supports and muslin hangings. Or, perhaps, a minimal futon mattress, a functional painted pine surround, or a no-nonsense divan. If, however, your bed frame is boring or unattractive, consider disguising it with plump padding and a fabric that feels heavenly next to bare skin – such as the soft jumbo cord shown opposite. The softened outlines can be emphasised with layers of throws, blankets, pillows and cushions, made from suede, chunky wool knits, fur, chenille or fleece. The overriding factor must be that they're cosy, warm and comfortable.

Flexible storage

Adequate storage is vital in a bedroom if you're to avoid distracting clutter. Built-in wardrobes and drawers can be tailor-made to your requirements; if you prefer a more eclectic look, however, you might want to mix individual items. A bedside table with several sizeable drawers, for example, can hide a lot of necessary but unattractive bits and pieces, and be a good-looking piece in its own right – a curving French antique, maybe, with a roughly distressed paint finish or even some gilding. Or you could opt for an open display of linens or clothing hanging from a wooden ladder or a functional but attractive metal rack – though this may take some discipline to keep looking tidy. Boxes or baskets, in plastic, wicker, canvas, metal or leather, can be chosen to emphasise the room's textural theme or to contrast with it, while changing the handles on drawers and wardrobes (you might like brushed stainless steel, faceted glass or leather straps) may be the finishing touch that transforms a pleasant bedroom into a really stunning one.

soft sensuality

For a bedroom that's irresistibly welcoming and luxurious, create a textural scheme that consists mostly of warm, pliable, and pampering fabrics, such as suede, silk, wool and leather. It's old-fashioned comfort given a modern twist.

Bedroom textures

KNITTING Knitted fabrics – whether delicate and sheer, or bold and chunky – make deliciously traditional bed throws and cushion covers.	**123**	**COWHIDE** A hide rug, cushion or even beanbag cover would make a funky yet comfortable addition to a contemporary bedroom.	**234**
SUEDE Natural suede is expensive, but you only need to use a little – perhaps as a cushion panel or footstool upholstery – for it to be very effective.	**224**	**WOOL CARPET** Though its colour is pleasantly neutral, there's plenty of textural interest in the tufted weave of this woollen carpet.	**256**
VELVET This velvet has a soft pile, a pleasant sheen, and a subtly ribbed surface texture – just right for a bedroom.	**200**	**MOIRE SILK** This smooth, cool, and slightly crunchy texture creates an elegant, classic effect.	**187**

▲ The right accessories enhance the textural theme of a country kitchen: huge ceramic jars, antique wooden stools, and copper pans are highly suitable

Rustic charm

A TIMELESS COMBINATION OF SEASONED TIMBER, BARE BRICK
AND WORN TILES ALWAYS EVOKES A WELCOMING ATMOSPHERE.
THIS LOOK OFFERS OLD-FASHIONED SIMPLICITY, GENUINE
PRACTICALITY AND CLASSIC, HOMELY COMFORT.

● Classic appliances suit a country kitchen perfectly, while chopped logs, hanging pans and a tiled work surface add textural interest.

▼ Though an old dresser might feature rugged, worn timber, a new one can show off equally interesting textures such as acid-etched glass or inlaid woods.

For a kitchen in truly traditional style, choose a palette of unpretentious materials which have character and attractive authenticity. On the far left, rough brick walls have been combined with a tough quarry-tiled floor in a similar warm earthy colour, though with a soft sheen to the pitted surface; the room is held together by a strong framework of roughly cut, scarred wooden beams. The overall result is an appealing unevenness, a rugged, 'country' effect that ignores fads and fancies in favour of basic function and charmingly natural good looks.

Inviting textures

Interestingly, there's very little paintwork in this room. Instead, the walls behind the work surfaces have been covered with small, hand-made ceramic tiles, their creamy, dimpled finish softly glazed for a slight shiny effect, while the panelled-pine cupboards have been left bare to show off the grain of the wood. It would be equally effective, in creating a room such as this, to use an old-fashioned wall treatment such as distemper or milk paint: the resulting soft, slightly mottled surface would complement the mix of rustic textures that gives the kitchen its warm, friendly feel.

It's essential to plan storage carefully in a country-style kitchen. Hide modern appliances behind cupboard doors, while retaining open storage – shelving, plate racks, hooks, a mobile butcher's block – to display copper kettles, cast-iron pans, glass storage jars, ceramic dishes, and wicker baskets. For maximum versatility and the beauty of traditional craftsmanship, consider installing a dresser: old or new, it's the perfect addition to this type of scheme.

ic charm

Unpretentious, straightforward materials such as terracotta, wood and wool create the right background textures for a country-style kitchen that has instinctive and enduring appeal.

Kitchen textures

578 TERRACOTTA FLOORING
Worn terracotta floors, or reclaimed tiles, are found in many period kitchens.

408 PATTERNED GLASS
Patterned glass makes an interesting door panel in kitchen units or a dresser.

246 TEXTURED RUG
Used on a hard kitchen floor, a textured cotton rug adds softness.

112 COMBED PAINTWORK
Two layers of paint in different colours, the top layer combed when wet, creates this informal effect.

490 WEATHERED WOOD
When designing a rustic kitchen, old wood is a good choice as it offers just the right textural style.

523 TRELLIS
Fit trellis into door panels instead of glass, or use it to train indoor climbing plants.

swatch

Uniquely individual

FOR A KITCHEN THAT'S FULL OF CHARACTER,
AVOID FITTED UNITS IN FAVOUR OF INFORMAL,
FREE-STANDING FURNITURE. AS FOR TEXTURES,
CHOOSE NATURAL WOOD, SOFTLY BUFFED METAL
AND WOVEN WICKER TO PROVIDE SURFACES THAT
ARE FULL OF VITALITY AND INTEREST.

Why settle for a bland, standard kitchen when you could have one that's unusual and beautiful? Long runs of rectangular boxes may be convenient, but they're not necessarily the most attractive choice: often a combination of fitted and unfitted pieces is best, with conventional units making the most of space (and hiding appliances such as dishwashers and washing machines), and more eclectic pieces adding a touch of personality with their different shapes, textures and colours.

In the pretty kitchen on the left, for example, a hanging pot rack, free-standing work surface and open plate rack are highly practical but also aesthetically pleasing, allowing displays of smooth ceramics, shiny metal implements and wicker baskets. If you have a low ceiling or limited floor space a ceiling rack or butcher's block may not be possible, but removing just one wall unit would create enough room for a storage shelf, rail or rack – even an old flowerpot filled with wooden spoons, or an enamel jug containing fresh flowers, will liven up a dull work surface.

Be creative

Another way to personalise your space is to think laterally. A solid-wood table like the one on the right, for instance, could be topped with a metal panel, and storage could rang from oversized boxes made from the palest new wood to containers in antique wood, leather, or even recycled rubber. Wooden or wicker bowls, raffia or bamboo place mats, simple ceramic crockery and elegant, traditional glassware would all make beautiful accessories, and a modern metal pendant lamp could be just the thing as a lively yet functional finishing touch.

◀ The neutral colours and natural textures of grainy wood, creamy paintwork and unglazed floor tiles are ideal as a background to a delightfully pretty but also practical room.

▶ Layers of texture in neutral colours ma for a simple and highly attractive table setti

uniquely individual

These textures are simple and natural, with a timeless quality that would enable them to fit into either a classic or modern scheme.

Kitchen textures

MATT EMULSION
For a calm, contemplative setting, paint kitchen walls with a pale, soft, matt color such as ivory, white or cream.

2

COTTON TICKING
A classic and inexpensive fabric, cotton ticking is durable, washable and attractive without being at all fussy.

159

BASKETWEAVE
'Country' chairs can be used in all but the most avant-garde of kitchen schemes.

293

OAK BOARDS
Floorboards made from solid oak have a character and integrity all their own. The more worn they are, the nicer they look.

505

POLISHED LIMESTONE
Like oak, a limestone floor will age naturally and has an intriguing patina that provides a wonderful textural base to a room.

527

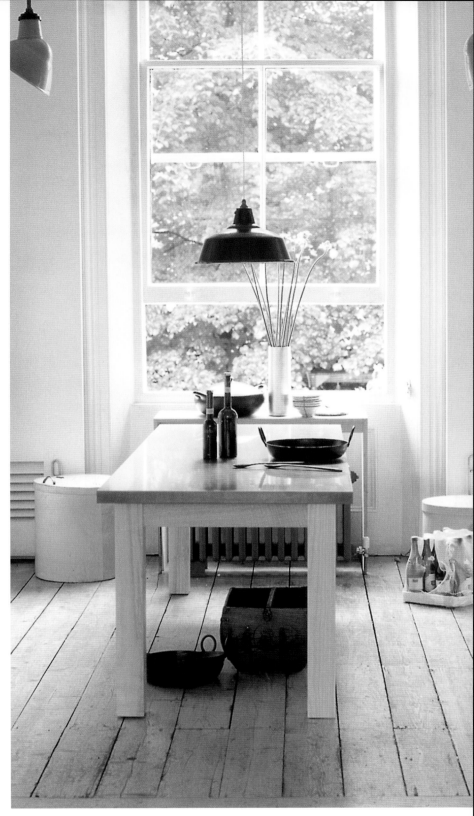

🔺 A casual dining table doubles as a food preparation area in this bright and airy kitchen. The different types of wood used have their own textures and characters, but the overall look is relaxed and inviting.

Fashion statement

GIVE A CONTEMPORARY DINING AREA A FUNKY
EDGE BY USING COLOURS, SHAPES AND TEXTURES IN
UNUSUAL WAYS – FROM A STATEMENT-MAKING FLOOR
TO THE SMALLEST OF ACCESSORIES, A LITTLE LATERAL
THINKING ALWAYS HAS FABULOUS RESULTS.

Some of the most successful room schemes start with a classic outlook and then develop a modern twist: a wooden dining table, for example, but in deep black wenge wood rather than the expected pine or oak; a storage cabinet, but made of galvanised steel and metal mesh rather than the standard timber; or a set of comfortable chairs, but in flexible, opaque plastic instead of the usual fabric upholstery. Surprise touches can be taken to extremes or kept as a restrained, barely noticeable element: used carefully, they can either update or radically alter a room. You could, for example, simply add felt place mats to a traditional table setting, or go the whole way and cover the floor of a conservatory-style dining room with smooth, round pebbles.

▼ A pebble floor might be hard on the feet but it certainly brings a feel of the outdoors to a conservatory-style dining room.

Shine on

In a bright and airy dining room you can make the most of light by using textures that are glossy and reflective. The floor in this cool, open-plan area consists of limewashed wooden boards, sealed with polyurethane varnish that gives them a soft glow while allowing the grain to show through; the table has a satiny, polished finish and the classic glassware and cutlery add sparkle. The rough place mats are the ideal counterpoint to these shiny surfaces, while the upmarket plastic chairs add another element – smooth yet matt in texture. All this, with just two basic colours, off-white and chocolate-brown, and a pleasing contrast of straight lines and curves: the result is a harmony of elements that's energising, out of the ordinary and up to the minute.

fashion statement

A dining room with real ambience and vitality needs several
interesting textures – not necessarily funky, but demonstrating an
unusual touch and some considered planning. Think carefully about
ways to give a classic look an unconventional twist.

Dining room textures

PEBBLES
Real pebbles as a flooring
are best kept outside.
Indoors, create a dramatic
effect with photographic
vinyl floor tiles.
350

FELT
Felt is a versatile material
that looks good in modern
and traditional settings.
Use it for cushion covers,
place mats or throws.
134

POLISHED WALNUT
Natural wood always makes
a good impression. The
dramatic grain of this
beautiful polished walnut
is a case in point.
509

METAL MESH
Silvery woven metal has an
eye-catching texture. Use
for door panels, shutters,
or underneath a glass-
topped table.
458

▲ This modern version of a traditional
doctor's cabinet is an ideal place to
store and display glassware.

► The contrasts of colour, texture and s▮
in this appealing dining roo▮
exciting but not too s▮

Metallic magic

USE METALS IN THE KITCHEN FOR A LOOK THAT CAN BE EITHER FUNKY AND
FUTURISTIC OR ELEGANTLY TIMELESS. PALE COLOURS AND SMOOTH, SHINY
SURFACES WILL, HOWEVER, ALWAYS POSSESS CONTEMPORARY APPEAL.

◀ A daring combination of terrazzo, marble, metal and glass makes no concession to tradition. The look is sleek, hi-tech and ultra-modern.

▶ Stainless-steel kitchen equipment always looks good, as well as being practical and long-lasting.

▲ A simple combination of two types of texture can have really attractive results. Here, the mix of wood and metal is well balanced, as is the use of fitted and unfitted pieces, and concealed and open storage.

Versatile and interesting, metal makes a good choice for a kitchen, whether it be as a fully fitted, professional-quality stainless-steel version, or simply employed in the form of a few good-looking accessories. Tough, durable and easy to maintain, it can be combined with other materials for a wide range of effects.

Use with wood, for example, and you temper its inherent hardness to create a warmer and more homely look, whether rustic, chic or, as seen in this kitchen on the left, enduringly classic. Wooden floorboards and a plain, solid timber table are the basis for a gathering of eclectic metal pieces, from work surface to chairs, storage to fridge-freezer, and even the dustbin and toaster. The simplicity of the texture and colour combinations prevents the room from seeming too hard or stark, and gives it great appeal.

Space-age catering

Mixing glass, marble and terrazzo with metal will make for an undeniably modern look – or even, as with the unusual, pod-like kitchen on the far left, give a space-age, just-about-to-take-off feel. With a preponderance of hard, smooth, shiny surfaces – especially the terrazzo floor and marble work surface – a kitchen such as this would not suit everyone; but even in neutral metallics, glass and greys, it's impressively bold and dazzling.

If you like the look of metal in a kitchen, but would prefer to introduce greater textural variety, consider rougher, softer and more three-dimensional materials. Take your pick from chairs made of matt plastic, frosted-glass cupboard fronts, displays of matt or glazed crockery, wicker storage baskets or paper lampshades, for example.

allic magic

Hard, hi-tech surfaces go together to make cool, contemporary kitchens. Their impact can be amazing, though if you want to tone it down a little incorporate some classic textures.

Kitchen textures

337 | **LINOLEUM FLOORING**
It looks like stone, but it's lino – inexpensive, softer underfoot, but less durable.

508 | **MAPLE WOOD**
The texture of this floor is warm and comfortable – tempering the harsher look of metal and glass.

460 | **METAL MESH**
This metal mesh has a fabulous three-dimensional texture - ideal for panels.

424 | **METAL TILES**
Embossed metal tiles such as these have a sculptural, quite clinical, modern look.

406 | **TEXTURED GLASS**
This texture would complement both hard and soft surfaces.

313 | **PLEATED RICE PAPER**
Space-age kitchens would benefit from futuristic fabrics for fittings such as blinds.

swatch

hi-tech haven

For a sleek and modern bathroom, look out for the hard, cold, smooth and reflective textures of metal, glass and stone.

Bathroom textures

ALUMINIUM
Use metal treadplate to cover floors or clad walls, though check with your retailer how best to seal it against damp.

474

FLECKED WEAVE
A simple blind at a bathroom window adds necessary softness, offsetting the harder textures elsewhere.

177

TEXTURED GLASS
What could be more appropriate for a bathroom shower panel than bubble-effect glass?

407

PATTERNED METAL
Metal can be treated in many different ways – take a trip to a metal fabricators to get an idea of the range available.

467

MOSAIC TILES
Mosaic can be bright and patterned or have a subtle effect. These pearlescent tiles would suit a contemporary bathroom.

435

MARBLE FLOORING
A marble-tiled floor is a luxurious choice. Though an ancient material, it is equally effective in a modern setting.

573

▶ It can be hard to introduce textural variety to a bathroom, but this combination of wood, glass, metal and ceramic tiles is a good example of how to do it.

▶ White paint, white towels and white fittings emphasize the gleaming metal, sleek glass and polished wood in this airy bathroom.

Hi-tech haven

SMOOTH, SHINY SURFACES EPITOMISE A MODERN
BATHROOM. YOU CAN SOFTEN THIS LOOK, HOWEVER,
WITH COLOURED CANDLES, PRETTY CERAMICS AND,
OF COURSE, PILES OF THICK TOWELS.

Hard textures are usually prevalent in a bathroom, and the obvious starting points for a contemporary design are the durable, easy-to-clean surfaces of ceramic, glass, chrome and stainless steel. Ceramic tiles or stone slabs are ideal for floors, though underfloor heating would make your feet cosier; alternatives include wood, perhaps coloured and laid in interesting patterns, as in the bathroom on the far left, or vinyl, which comes in convincing wood- or stone-effect. Continue the ceramic theme around the bath or shower, using either standard-sized tiles or smaller mosaic ones. The latter create an interesting yet subtle effect, which could be heightened by the use of a darker grout.

A stainless-steel handbasin with exposed waste pipe gives a chic, industrial feel. You can also buy stainless-steel lavatories, and even baths – though the cumulative effect might be a little too institutional! Other options would be a chrome laundry bin and heated towel rail. Such reflective surfaces make the room seem more spacious and emphasise its role as one of cleansing and refreshing.

In the clear

Glass is a fabulous material to use in a bathroom. A huge shower door made from translucent glass gives a barely there impression, while glass shelves appear to float and, again, maximise a sense of space; frosted, etched or coloured glass are alternatives. To continue this look, you could also use stacked-up acrylic storage boxes, neatly holding all those bathroom odds and ends.

Without a little soft texture, however, a hi-tech bathroom might be attractive to look at but would be unpleasant to use. Take the edge off the clinical atmosphere with a few carefully chosen accessories and, of course, piles of towels: in a plain colour and neatly folded they'll still appear tidy and practical, but will also add that touch of human comfort that's absolutely vital.

◄ **Though tiny, this room has been very carefully planned to include an interesting mix of materials. The glass shelf across the base of the window is an especially nice touch.**

THE WARMTH AND HONESTY OF WOOD CREATE AN ATMOSPHERE THAT'S WELCOMING, COMFORTABLE AND DOWN-TO-EARTH. FOR AN APPEALING ORIENTAL STYLE, STICK TO SIMPLE SHAPES, COOL COLOURS AND THE MINIMUM OF ACCESSORIES.

Oriental simplicity

◑ In an Eastern-style bathroom, as above right, bamboo furniture is especially appropriate. And large, woven-grass baskets provide both useful storage space and fabulous rough, hairy texture.

◑ As a contrast to the warmth of wood, a minimal towel radiator is cool, smooth and sleek.

A sizeable bathroom that's kept clear of clutter has a wonderfully calm and relaxing feel – make the most of the fact that large areas of floor and walls are visible by choosing materials that are texturally interesting. Wooden floorboards, as seen here, are ideal; there is a variety of options, however: they could be new or reclaimed, varnished matt or glossy, laid parallel to the walls or diagonally. You could even paint over them with hard-wearing floor paint. Walls could be covered with matt emulsion for a smooth, sophisticated effect, though a rougher plaster finish might have more impact. For a truly Eastern style, they could be lacquered with high-gloss varnish, though you do need perfect walls to make this treatment look really impressive.

Bathing beauty

Wooden tongue-and-groove, often found as wall panelling in bathrooms, can also be used, as in the room on the right, to clad the sides of the bath. If you want to go the whole way, install a deep Japanese bath made completely of wood: it will undoubtedly be the focal point of the room. To create this overall look, you need to add very little else: perhaps some free-standing storage or a screen; a simple mirror; a rail or shelf on which to place towels; and a few accessories, made of wood, leather, canvas, bamboo, woven grass or understated chrome. As long as the shapes and textures of the objects are interesting, maintaining a slightly bare aesthetic is ideal.

oriental simplicity

Never underestimate the appeal of utter simplicity. Sometimes luxury comes from thoughtful planning, careful execution and the use of honest, straightforward materials. Buy the best you can afford, and mix with inexpensive items such as canvas and paper.

Bathroom textures

ROUGH PLASTER
The pleasant texture of a roughly plastered wall provides a good background for smoother fittings in an unpretentious bathroom.
481

PAPER WEAVE
This loosely woven fabric has a decidedly oriental appearance and would fit well into this type of scheme.
301

TROPICAL HARDWOOD
Dark and distinctive hardwoods such as this, used sparingly, create a dramatic, Eastern-style effect.
494

CHECKERBOARD SISAL
The weave of this natural fibre flooring is unusual in that it's flatter than most. It makes a good alternative to wooden flooring.
283

CANVAS FABRIC
You can't find fabric that's much cheaper or more simple than this. It's tough and hard-wearing, and has a pleasant, flecked texture.
214

BAMBOO BOARDS
Bamboo floorboards have an unusual grain and a delightful colour; they are, of course, perfect for an Eastern-style bathroom.
507

◑ The elegance of wood contrasts with the rough surface of the plastered walls in the fabulously bright and spacious room

swatch

A MARBLE BATHROOM COMBINES ELEGANT, UPMARKET
LOOKS WITH SUPERB PRACTICALITY AND DURABILITY. IT'S
SUBTLE YET INTRIGUING, RESTFUL YET EFFICIENT –
A SCHEME THAT COMBINES THE BEST OF OLD AND NEW
FOR THE ULTIMATE TIMELESS ATTRACTION.

Traditional values

△ A Roman-style mosaic pattern made from small, matt marble tiles gives a bathroom a feel that is at once traditional and very up to date.

When designing a marble bathroom, be careful the result isn't too hard and unforgiving – the key is to bring in shape colours and textures that add understated personality. As the stone itself will be dominant, choose a version that suit the size of the room: a very strong pattern may look fabulo in a large room but create too much of an impact in a small one, for example. And don't just think of the pattern but als of the texture, which could be honed to a shiny finish, give an 'eggshell' surface or left slightly matt. You can also creat interest by setting smaller tiles of dark marble or slate into a floor made of large marble slabs, or by laying marble mosai as shown to great effect in the bathroom shown on the left.

Perfect partners

Mirror, wood, metal and ceramic are natural complements t marble. A large mirrored panel, cut to fit a whole wall, is impressive, contemporary and useful; or a smaller, oval mirror, perhaps with a carved and gilded wooden frame, could be hung over a washbasin for a more classic effect. Taps made of metal (ranging from chrome to brass) can be chosen to reiterate your style, whether traditional or trendy and you may want to add further metal touches such as a soap dish or storage canisters. Ceramic pots, dishes and hand-made tiles, glazed matt or shiny, give an impression o thoughtful individuality, and the entire look can be completed by adding softer counterpoints, in the form of a fabric shower curtain (lined with plastic), a few towels and bath mat made of fluffy cotton or woven wicker.

○ Hand-made ceramic tiles have a pleasantly uneven appearance and offer a subtle appeal.

○ Smooth, hard and cold, marble and mirror are complemented by the warmer, gentler texture of natural wood in this airy and interesting bathroom.

Bathrooms are often based around hard surfaces, but vary their textures and the overall scheme can still be interesting and enjoyable.

Bathroom textures

MARBLE MOSAIC
Small marble tiles create a pleasant surface when laid all in one colour, or can be arranged in an infinite variety of decorative patterns.

443

MARBLE SLAB
The graphic patterning of grey-and-white marble always looks smart. Its unique look fits in with all sorts of schemes, whether classic or contemporary.

560

COMPOSITE STONE TILES
Unconventional floorings such as this brick-effect stone would look marvellous in a neutral bathroom.

587

PEWTER FINISH PAINT EFFECT
If marble is simply too expensive, create eye-catching walls either with a mould-resistant wallpaper or an unusual paint effect.

120

POLISHED PLASTER
A plaster render like this (properly sealed against damp) has a rough, authentic aesthetic that can tone down smoother, more polished elements in a room.

483

○ A set of ceramic containers in varying sizes provides organised storage that also features soft colour and an intriguing texture.

45

A BRIGHT, UNCLUTTERED LOOK MAKES A HOME OFFICE A PLACE WHERE YOU'LL ACTIVELY WANT TO SPEND YOUR TIME. PLAIN AND SIMPLE COLOURS AND TEXTURES HELP CREATE AN ATMOSPHERE THAT'S CONDUCIVE TO WORK YET STILL ENJOYABLE.

Form and function

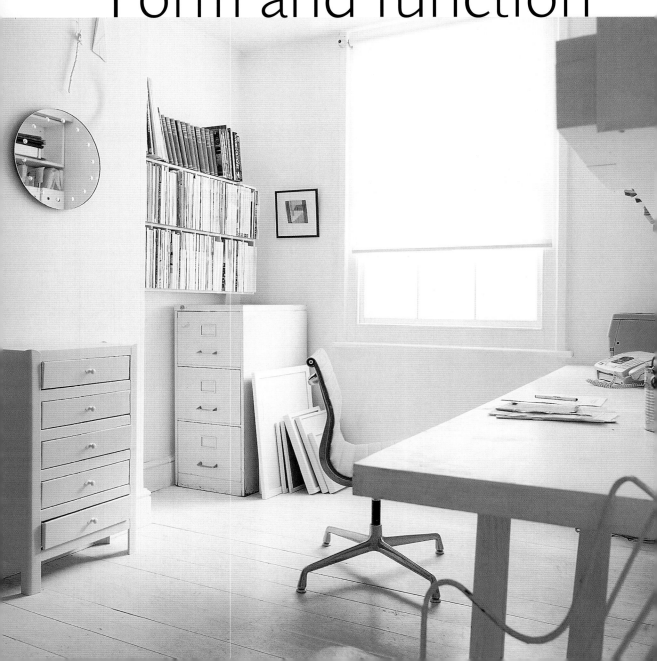

❯ Don't overlook the possibilities for textural interest even in such apparently mundane objects as office shelving and storage boxes.

A good office chair is vital. ⌐ose one that's sturdy, ⌐fortable and adjustable: this ⌐mple is all three, and its soft ⌐ding makes a nice contrast ⌐he harder elements used ⌐where in the room.

Whether you use a workroom at home to write letters, sit at a computer, sew drapes or type up accounts, there's no reason why it should be dull and uninteresting. It must be practical, of course, but it stands to reason that the more pleasant your surroundings, the more productive and efficient you'll be at your work.

Home offices in neutral colours tend to be calm and contemplative, and using plenty of white or very pale colours emphasises natural light. The all-white office shown on the far left, for example, contains plenty of efficient storage, and a lack of clutter helps to increase its bright, spacious feel. Without the distraction of mess or lots of clashing colours it would be easy to get down to work in here – even the various textural elements used in the room have been carefully co-ordinated to minimise visual disturbance. From the soft matt walls to the satiny floor, the sheer blind to the limed-wood tabletop, they gently complement each other without fuss or confusion.

Adding to the atmosphere

The accessories you choose can make a huge difference to the look and feel of a workroom. In the main picture, for example, a mirror-faced clock, brushed-metal lampshade and ridged tin-can pen holders add elements of textural contrast; their informal appearance suits this room well. You could include storage in the form of tall metal shelves, as seen on the left, or take a businesslike approach with the addition of, say, a sleek, modern desk lamp and co-ordinating necessities such as box files, pen trays, pencil sharpeners, staplers and hole punchers. Of course, if you were tired of neutrals, this is your chance to add bold impact and a splash of colour in the form of office essentials in bright, cheerful and invigorating shades.

form and function

Avoid distractions in a home office by choosing textures that are quiet and simple, yet attractive and appealing. Try a mixture of matte emulsion, leather, wool, felt, paper and sophisticated linen.

Home office textures

WHITE PAINT
Nothing could be simpler and more straightforward than ⌐sing plain white emulsion on ⌐alls for a subtle background.
1

GALWAY LINEN
This linen has a subtle weave that makes it a comfortable addition to an understated office.
183

NATURAL LEATHER
A good chair can be the focus of a home office, especially when the surroundings are plain. Cover it in leather for sophisticated impact.
226

FINE WOOL CARPET
This carpet is soft underfoot without being too luxurious. Its ribbed texture makes a change from loops or cut pile.
270

THICK FELT
Soft and warm, felt adds an unexpected but extremely welcome texture to a home working environment.
137

TEXTURED WALLPAPER
If you feel your walls need slightly more than plain white paint, consider textured wallpaper.
312

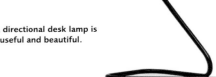

▲ A directional desk lamp is both useful and beautiful.

Back to basics

◆ A classic table lamp such as this is ideal with a traditional-style desk.

▶ The agreeable hairy roughness of coir matting creates a friendly feel here – it's inexpensive and durable, too.

GET AWAY FROM THE STRESSES OF A MODERN WORKING LIFE WITH A HOME OFFICE THAT HAS EVERY TRADITIONAL COMFORT. YOU CAN CREATE A RELAXING ATMOSPHERE YET STILL ENJOY THE BENEFITS OF MODERN TECHNOLOGY.

The basics for a functional home office are a spacious desk that's at the right height for you, a comfortable chair, adequate storage and good lighting; though if you don't spend hours in the office then you needn't worry about the chair being infinitely adjustable, and a traditional-style lamp may be just as good as a flexible, hinged-arm type. Consider what works best for you, remembering that you can always hide a modern fax or answering machine inside an antique cabinet, and that it's easily possible to make an office really homely by incorporating a fireplace, pictures on the walls, old-fashioned telephone and plenty of ornaments. A squashy couch piled up with soft cushions and throws may be just the place for quiet contemplation, and an assortment of books will look especially nice on open shelving.

Gentle contrasts

Making good use of texture will really bring this sort of room to life: your aim is to create a cosy, welcoming feel by using robust, natural materials. Avoid the overly modern look of plastic, rubber or stainless steel; instead think of contrasting rough and smooth, hard and soft in a gentle, unimposing way by using coir flooring, tactile rugs – perhaps made of natural hide or wool with a deep, giving pile – old wood (for panelling walls or as a desk with brass-handled drawers) and accessories in leather, paper, suede or matt metal.

A silk shade combined with a ceramic lamp base is one good choice for lighting, while another would be a brass base with a frosted glass shade; as with other furnishings in this type of scheme, they both offer a satisfying combination of textures together with absolute practicality and a suitably familiar, classic design.

▲ String has been glued in patterns to the surface of this timber desk, and makes an intriguing and exciting texture.

◀ Storage boxes made of leather have an air of quiet sophistication.

to basics

rround yourself ith traditional mforts and make a ork space that's elcoming and joyable to be in. mbine classic od and leather th the more ntemporary looks

Home office textures

234   **COWHIDE**
Funky but functional, this rug will update any room and makes for a dynamic office.

SISAL CARPET
Sisal flooring is ideal for a home office – durable, easy to clean, and good-looking in an understated way

227   **PIERCED LEATHER**
Leather – even when pierced – is upmarket, comfortable and timeless.

SOFT LAMBSWOOL
The soft and fluffy bouclé texture of this woollen fabric is unexpected, yet ideal for an office

167   **TEXTURED COTTON**
A classic woven cotton complements a range of other textures.

EXOTIC WOOD
Tropical hardwood gives the impression of high quality and enduring luxury

swatch

Soft

SOFT COLOURS ARE **EASY** TO PUT TOGETHER, AND ALWAYS **CREATE** HARMONIOUS, WELCOMING AND RELAXING SCHEMES. USE THEM TO HIGHLIGHT **GENTLE** CONTRASTS AND COMBINATIONS OF TEXTURES TO **DELIGHTFUL** EFFECT.

colours

SOFT COLOURS

◀ **A combination of several muted colours is calm and pretty in this light-filled dining area.**

▼ **Using peach-coloured paintwork with an aluminium floor might be unexpected, but it's certainly effective.**

The attraction of using soft colours is that they are gentle, easy to live with and straightforward to combine in pleasing ways. Think of the colours of an English country garden – lavender, hollyhocks, foxgloves, delphiniums, roses and sweet peas – what could be nicer? There's nothing strident or disturbing here; in fact, this type of scheme can be very calming: good for the soul as much as for the eyes.

Soft colours include knocked-back versions of primaries in the form of pink, baby blue and lemon yellow, and pale secondary shades such as lilac, mint green and peach. Of course, there may only be a subtle difference between a pink that is soft and a pink that is strong; the key is to choose shades that won't dazzle or demand too much, but that simply contribute to the room's overall harmony. And, while a scheme could be based completely around one soft colour, two together, or indeed several, there's nothing wrong with adding a bolder shade for extra emphasis (think of the impression you could make by combining fuchsia with lilac and pale pink, for example, or turquoise with watery blue and lemon) or using neutral colours as a background. Metal surfaces, especially brushed stainless steel, and pale, grained woods look particularly good when combined with soft colourways. That's the great thing about soft shades: you can do almost anything you like with them and they still look fabulous.

Natural materials can make a good starting point for a soft colour scheme: it's surprising how many of them come in gentle but colourful shades. Slate, for example, usually thought of as grey, can also be tinged a delicate pink, purple or green, while marble and terrazzo offer a wealth of lovely colours. Plaster, too, either in its natural pink or in tinted form, has a soft tone that's highly attractive. Coloured glassware and ceramic tiles, crockery or vases make a wonderful basis for decorating in soft colours, while textiles, carpets and rugs can contribute enormously to a delightful scheme such as this.

△ A fake fur throw provides a luscious counterpoint on a traditional couc
Here, roughly textured wood and industrial metal add an informal fee

Timeless good taste

THE GENTLE CALMNESS OF SOFT COLOURS CAN GIVE
A LIVING ROOM ENORMOUS APPEAL. MAKE THE
MOST OF TACTILE MATERIALS BY CREATING A LOOK
THAT'S LUXURIOUS YET UNCLUTTERED, WITH POISE,
CLASS AND QUIET SOPHISTICATION.

One way to approach the design of a living room is to base it around a beautiful fabric in a cool, muted shade. The fabric could be used for drapes or furniture, a throw or even a wall-hanging. You can then choose other colours, textures and materials that bring out its best qualities. These two traditional couches, for example, have been covered in a linen/cotton fabric that is hard-wearing and highly attractive, smooth yet with a noticeable crisp weave.

Layer upon layer

Having chosen a main fabric, the next step is to build up the different textures around it, bearing in mind that this look requires a minimum of decorative flourishes and absolutely no fussy details. It may be best to keep walls pale and quite smooth in order to provide a quiet background against which everything else will stand out. On the floor, rough boards washed with thinned-down white paint give a casual, off-the-cuff flourish, while smooth, shiny parquet has a more upmarket air. Or you could try a wool carpet, sisal flooring, or even rubber or metal floor tiles.

Finally, add tufted, woven or shagpile rugs, and one or two pieces of furniture, perhaps made from worn, reclaimed wood or gleaming glass. Don't forget lamps: in traditional ceramic, glass with paper or silk, or workmanlike metal. Throws and cushions could be in the same fabric as the couch with unusual buttons or a pretty trimming, or in a different fabric entirely, providing a glamorous contrast.

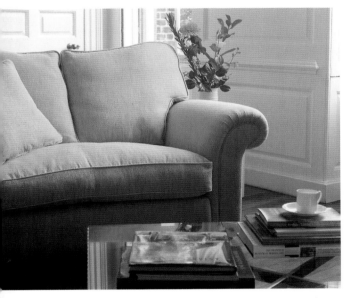

● The textures in this room have been subtly contrasted. Apart from the slightly ugh weave of the couch fabric, everything is smooth and shiny in varying degrees.

ess
taste

tural materials
ch as wood, hide
d muslin are the
sics for a living
om scheme that is
lm and quiet. Their
xtures are
autifully
mplementary and

Living room textures

515 RED OAK FLOORING
Timber floors look good, last well, and wear beautifully – a perennial favorite.

236 GOATSKIN
Soft and shaggy, a furry throw or rug (real or fake) adds a cosy touch.

281 RIBBED SISAL
This rough, hairy flooring brings softer textures into focus.

SHEER MUSLIN
A delicate cotton muslin – here in an unusual apple green – is a good choice for

SOFT CHENILLE
An appealing fabric for upholstery or drapes, chenille is irresistibly tactile

MARBLED PAPER
This wallpaper is a subtle and upmarket option for a traditional

swatch

Forces of nature

BE INSPIRED BY NATURAL SHADES AND CREATE A FRESH LOOK FOR A LIVING ROOM. NEITHER TRADITIONAL NOR TRENDY, GENTLE COLOURS AND TEXTURES WORK TOGETHER EFFORTLESSLY AND HAVE A TIMELESS, ENDURING APPEAL.

A living room designed around a natural theme is delightfully pretty – as can be seen in the relaxed, comfortable room shown in the main picture. When putting together such a scheme, find colours that complement each other in an interesting, but not too dramatic, way. It may help to think of the seasons: warm russets and browns for autumn, deeper reds and aubergines for winter, fresh limey yellows and greens for spring, and pretty lavender, sky blue and pink for summer.

Transformation time

You'll find that textures for this scheme follow on quite readily. Again, take as your starting point the natural world and note the wonderful variety that you could introduce: perhaps woven willow, tree bark, birds' eggs, soft fur, rounded pebbles or worn stone, to name but a few. In this scheme, the basic textures are the ribbed carpet and a wall painted a pale pastel-green. The main item of furniture, a two-seat couch, has been completely covered by a chenille throw. As well as introducing another textural element, this is an ideal way to disguise a chair or couch that's badly worn or doesn't fit into your colour scheme – but do ensure that your throw is large enough to cover the piece entirely, and tuck it well into the sides and back so it doesn't ruck up as soon as someone sits on it.

The finishing touches are some more cosy throws, cushions with textures that range from suede to smocking, and some carefully chosen accessories including a basketweave bag, crackleglaze vase, and paper lamp shade. As can be seen in the pictures top right and bottom left, thoughtful details such as a cushion made from an innovative fabric or a careful grouping of pretty ceramics can be incredibly effective. Without a doubt, this is a look that's inexpensive and easy to emulate.

---

swatch

forces of nature

From crunchy leaves and woven leather to grained wood and softly ribbed wool, the textures of nature can be combined and contrasted to create a delicious scheme for a living room.

Living room textures

FALL LEAVES
More or less any surface can be photographed and transferred onto vinyl floor tiles. These leaves look particularly effective.
351

SISAL CARPET
Natural fiber floorings are made in various weaves; this medium-ribbed version could be used almost anywhere in the house.
285

WOVEN LEATHER
Natural but still sophisticated, woven leather makes an ideal covering for a cushion in a scheme of this type.
225

MAPLE VENEER
Veneer panels, though not inexpensive, make a superb covering for a wall – or maybe just a small section of a wall.
512

MATTE PAINT
Choose a soft, fresh color of matte paint, distemper or milk paint with which to cover one or more walls.
49

RIBBED WOOL
This woolen fabric echoes the sisal carpet, but makes a nice complement as it's soft and giving rather than rough and hairy.
131

▶ Matt on matt – the muted colour and texture of these bottle-shaped vases, set against a painted fire surround, make a delightful and subtle combination.

▶ Against the background of a smooth, matt-painted wall, there is a range of warm, soft textures in this room. The small wooden cupboard with ribbed rattan doors makes an excellent, quiet counterpoint

This cushion fabric has a fabulous, unusual texture – it's emphasised by the smooth background of the chair fabric and a wall covered in large panels of beautiful, unpainted wood.

▲ An eclectic choice of textures works well in this fashion-conscious room.

Fresh vision

WHETHER YOU CHOOSE TRADITIONAL, CONTEMPORARY OR
UNUSUAL MATERIALS, A COMBINATION OF WARM, SOFT SHADES
WILL HELP CREATE A LIVING ROOM THAT'S FRIENDLY AND INVITING.

The colour family that stretches from red through pink to lilac and plum has instant human appeal, but the effects of individual shades can be very different. Rose pink and pale mauve, for example, are pretty and delicate; bubble gum and scarlet lively and invigorating; and the darker aubergine shades luxurious and cosy. Add to this the impact of form and texture and the results can be stunning.

Fashionable – and fun

In the modern room above, a designer chair upholstered in bold stretch fabric is the basis for a look that's eclectic and funky. The chair itself contrasts the matt softness of the textile with smooth, shiny metal, while the painted plaster walls feature a metal-trimmed display shelf; large vases in glass and acrylic add yet another texture to the mix. The overall result is bold and exciting, yet still easy to live with. Other materials that would work in this type of room might include rubber, plastic, vinyl, concrete, flokati and, if you like a no-holds-barred look, maybe even some whimsical ones such as bubble wrap and Astroturf.

For an even softer look, choose a classic designer chair upholstered in dark, intense leather, like the one in the modern living room on the right, which has a warmth and tactile quality that forces you to relax. The sumptuous nature of this comfortable corner is further emphasised by the deep-pile woolen rug and curving shapes of the chair and footstool, the wooden side table and acrylic magazine rack. It's a subtle, upmarket and informal combination of colour, shape and texture that creates an immediate, yet understated, impact.

fresh vision

By cleverly contrasting different textures, you can create rooms that are interesting both to look at and to live in.

Living room textures

FAKE LEATHER
Exciting and original in texture and colour, this fabric would be great for upholstery, cushions or a beanbag cover.

220

SHEEPSKIN
Soft, fluffy, and shaggy, sheepskin is attractive and looks good on wooden or natural fibre floors.

237

LINOLEUM FLOORING
Lino would probably not be most people's first choice for a living area, but with an interesting texture it can be highly effective.

343

TEXTURED GLASS
The opacity of glass means it's a good way to add texture without cluttering a room – ideal for shelving, bowls, or drinking glasses.

404

▼ This side table contrasts dark oak with clear glass set against smooth walls painted in warm, soft colors. The silver lining of the wooden bowl gives a modern twist to a classic accessory.

Wood, acrylic and shiny metal make a good contrast to the softness of leather and wool.

▲ Accessories such as ceramic bowls, wooden picture frames and, of course, fresh flowers really help to complete a sensual bedroom scheme

A calm retreat

SOFT COLOURS REALLY COME INTO THEIR OWN IN THE BEDROOM, WHERE THEY HELP TO SOOTHE AWAY THE STRESSES OF THE DAY. COMBINE WITH A VARIETY OF INTERESTING, LUXURIOUS TEXTURES TO CREATE AN INDULGENT HAVEN.

When you use generous amounts of fabric in a bedroom it results in a floaty, feminine look, particularly when colours are restricted to the paler end of the palette. Sheer muslin, or a gathered length of unbleached linen, looks fabulous at window (and lets in plenty of light), and it's easy to make drapes for a four-poster bed by sewing simple ties along or edge of a standard sheet or ready-made drape.

The plainest bed linen can be enlivened with subtle pipin

◀ These sheer drapes are made of wonderful metallic mesh fabric; their texture makes a fascinating contrast to that of the smooth glass bottle.

swatch

a calm retreat

Choose giving, informal textures with which to build up layers of luxury and create a bedroom that's sensuous, calming and relaxing.

Bedroom textures

BRUSHED PAINT EFFECT
A gentle paint effect can give a warmer impression than plain-painted walls, without being overbearing or intrusive.
107

THICK FELT
Though an inexpensive and utilitarian fabric, the thick, soft texture of felt creates an impression of attainable opulence.
135

SHEER DRAPES
Sheer fabric is pretty even when plain, but a small, sweet pattern can add decorative impact at the window.
147

WOOL BLANKET
Like felt, wool has eternal, old-fashioned appeal. Its warmth and comfort are always a benefit in a cosy bedroom.
243

BASKETWEAVE
Woven cane – for chair seats, blinds or wall coverings – has a charm and faintly rustic air that works in a peaceful room.
292

ELM WOOD
Classic bedroom furniture – made of beautiful, natural wood – is always a good partner to elegant and indulgent fabrics.
498

buttons, ties or borders, and you can add a touch of luxury with a casual throw or by adding piles of cushions made from soft, felted or knitted wool, velvet, cashmere, pashmina or silk satin.

Tactile patinas

If you're aiming for an informal, country look, a good complement to all this fabric would be to choose furniture and accessories made from harder, rougher wood and wicker. Wooden pieces, whether chests, beds, chairs, trays or bowls, could be precisely made, Shaker-style in maple or cherry, highly polished antique pieces, or beaten-up second-hand versions with a characterful patina; wicker baskets of all shapes and sizes come in a range of lovely, gentle colours and interesting weaves, while rounded wicker chairs always seem to fit well into this type of scheme.

On the floor, a soft carpet is kind to bare feet, or you could place a rug on top of either wooden boards – painted, stained, varnished or oiled – or a natural fibre floorcovering made from jute, sisal or seagrass. Walls could perhaps be bare brick, rough plaster or painted wooden panelling, while lighting is best kept low and romantic (though do remember to provide good directional light for mirrors and dressing areas), with lamps in a variety of shapes and sizes made from wood, ceramic, glass, paper, silk and raffia.

◀ Lidded wicker baskets are a good-looking method of storage. An alternative might be a large wooden chest which could, with a cushion on top, double as a seat.

Relaxed grandeur

USE ANTIQUE PIECES TO GIVE A BEDROOM A
SENSE OF OCCASION – COMBINED WITH MUTED
COLOURS AND TACTILE FABRICS THEY NEEDN'T
BE OVER-IMPOSING. YOU CAN COMBINE
COMFORT WITH A SURE SENSE OF STYLE.

The textures in a bedroom tend to be soft and smooth, warm and giving, which is ideal for creating an atmosphere of sensual relaxation. For variety and interest, however, it's good to include touches of harder or rougher textures.

In the striking green bedroom to the right, for example, a white carpet with a dense, low pile provides a forgiving base while the chaise-longue and bed are upholstered in luxurious velvet and padded cotton respectively. Pretty bed linen and sheer muslin drape over the headboard contribute to the overall effect of luxurious tranquillity.

Structured sensuality

The bed's carved wooden frame, however, together with the antique wardrobe and, especially, the metal corona above the head board, add a hard structure to the room that gives the design an interesting edge. The large mirror on the wardrobe is another pleasantly hard, smooth surface, with the added benefit of being placed opposite the window so as to reflect light into the room. Meanwhile, the metal lamp base echoes the form and material of the chandelier, but is downplayed by its plain paper shade.

Bed linen itself can also provide a variety of textures. Though sheets, pillowcases and duvet covers are usually made from plain cotton, polycotton or linen, they could have interesting edging, buttonholes or borders, and blankets, throws and cushions might be made from knitted chenille, thick soft wool, warm felt, fake fur, smooth silk or old-fashioned waffle.

swatch

relaxed grandeur

Rooms containing textures that are all too similar will inevitably be bland and boring. Mix hard and soft, rough and smooth materials with careful consideration to create a bedroom that has a sumptuous, sophisticated look and a relaxing, inviting feel.

Bedroom textures

WOVEN JACQUARD
Intricate and subtle, the textures of a self-coloured weave brings a tailored classicism to a bedroom scheme.

170

TEXTURED WALLPAPER
This smart wallpaper isn't overly eye-catching, but makes a pleasant textural change from smooth paintwork.
320

LIMED WOOD
Liming wood emphasises its grain and allows you to tone it gently with colours used elsewhere.

116

ROUGH PLASTER
Tinted and pitted plaster is another wall treatment that's unusual without being overbearing.
487

QUILTED VELVET
A strong diamond pattern distinguishes this fabric – it would be fantastic as a luxurious bed throw.

211

RUSH FLOORING
Softer underfoot than both sisal and coir, rush is a delightful flooring with an interesting woven texture.
280

▶ The ribbed texture of these throws and blankets would look great against a plain, smooth duvet cover.

▲ Used with plain walls and carpet as well as pretty textiles, the antique pieces in this room are attractive and comfortable without being awe-inspiring.

◀ Chambray bed linen made from a mix of cotton and polyester is both soft against the skin and easy to wash.

Light and inviting

A BEDROOM CAN BE WARM AND WELCOMING
WHILE STILL LOOKING FASHIONABLY MODERN. THE
KEY IS TO AVOID CLUTTER, USE PLAIN AND SIMPLE
FURNISHINGS AND CHOOSE PRETTY COLOURS
COMBINED WITH IRRESISTIBLE TEXTURES.

Sometimes just one gorgeous texture can have a big impact on a room, and in a bedroom the thing that usually stands out most is the bedcover. Choose one in a fairly subtle colour and it will emphasise a warm and cosy texture all the more – whether it be made of fleece, mohair, velvet, wool or silk. Match it with a few scatter cushions against smooth cotton or linen pillows and you'll create a beautiful basis around which to design the room.

Keep it simple

For this type of look the Mies van der Rohe dictum 'less is more' really applies. Stick to a few plain pieces, avoid decorative twiddles and twirls, aim for understated textures, and you'll actually create a greater impact. Paint walls in a muted matt emulsion and choose flooring for its subtle interest: sisal or coir matting, for example, or perhaps sanded-back (or painted) floorboards with a fake sheepskin rug, or even a low-pile carpet in a colour that tones with the walls. Keep your bed frame and all other furniture extremely simple. Minimal, square lines are best, and you might want to invest in one large piece of storage – a wooden chest, for example, or perhaps a long, box-shaped head board with a hinged lid – so that you can hide away anything that's unattractive and non-essential.

A fleece throw and cushions are the focus for a style that's [rel]axed and modern. Cotton bed linen makes a lovely contrast, as [do]es the mix of old and new wood, sisal flooring and glass vases.

◀ The raised height of these shelves makes the room seem larger. A fake sheepskin rug on a wooden floor is a classic combination of two wonderful textures.

You can vary the textures in a room such as this by introducing lighter, more translucent objects. Make a drape from a softly gathered length of sheer muslin hung from a metal or bamboo pole, add a paper table lamp or place some coloured glass vases on a bedside table. Keep your accessories to a minimum, however – a light touch is best for a bedroom that's both comfortable and contemporary.

light and inviting

Basic materials and unpretentious textures combine to create a bedroom that has simple style. There's no need to spend a great deal of money – inexpensive chipboard and paper can be just as effective as their more luxurious and expensive counterparts.

Bedroom textures

SHEEPSKIN
You could easily design a whole room around the delightful texture of this natural sheepskin.

237

PAPER
With a little imagination, you could put this woven paper fabric to many uses, from wall panels to lamp shades and picture frames.
310

CHIPBOARD
This wood may look a little unfinished unless you give it a coat of paint, or cover it with matt varnish to bring out its interesting texture.

518

CHENILLE
Soft, warm chenille is lovely as a bedcover, or can even be lightly gathered to make a pair of bedroom curtains.

207

▲ Paper lamps such as this are the epitome of simplicity and work well in a room where other textures are quite heavy and hard.

Sleek and chic

sleek and chic

Metals, stone and glass make a fabulous combination in a kitchen. Surfaces can vary from rough to smooth, flat to three-dimensional.

Kitchen textures

LAMINATED WORK SURFACE
Dark and mysterious, this marble-effect laminate more than matches its expensive stone competitors.
377

DIMPLED GLASS
The dramatic dimples in this coloured glass give it a wonderfully graphic quality. It's ideal for modern cupboard doors.
410

METAL FLOORING
The embossed patterns of metal sheeting make it a non-slip surface; it also adds another layer of texture to a room.
475

GLASS MOSAIC
Mosaic tiles are often used in bathrooms, but there's no reason why they shouldn't be laid as a kitchen splashback.
437

METAL MESH
A gold-coloured metal mesh in a cupboard door panel looks unusual and exciting, with a texture similar to that of knitting.
462

PITTED LIMESTONE
Pale stone floors lighten and brighten small kitchens. Though the slabs can be honed smooth, this rather tough texture is a pleasant antidote to smooth and shiny metal and glass.
529

○ Open shelves and hanging racks are a good way to display kitchen kit. Here, smooth stainless steel looks good against matt mosaic tiles.

Combining shiny steel with matt paintwork ɔws both elements to look their best.

A good balance of textural elements gives this kitchen dramatic impact. The nples on the cupboard doors echo the pierced metal mesh on the drawers.

ONCE THE PRESERVE OF THE PROFESSIONAL KITCHEN, METAL HAS NOW MADE IT INTO EVERYDAY HOMES. TEAM IT WITH PLAIN, PAINTED SURFACES FOR CONTEMPORARY CHIC, OR COMBINE WITH NATURAL WOOD AND STONE FOR A MORE LAID-BACK EFFECT.

The attraction of stainless steel lies in its simplicity and versatility, and it looks particularly lovely in a kitchen that features gentle colour. A long run of stainless-steel worktop looks gorgeous, and has a crisp, neat finish that's extremely satisfying. You can take this look further by adding a steel splashback, extractor hood, sink and cooking appliances, and even clever details such as a trim laminated onto the front edge of a shelf. Don't forget that zinc and aluminium are alternatives for a metal splashback. Smaller items, too, from taps to kettles, jugs to containers, can pick up the theme of shiny, metallic surfaces: handles, pulls and switches in a material such as brushed stainless steel are pleasantly tactile. And, if you want to be really adventurous, you could install a metal floor, or cover the front of your cabinets with a thin sheet of metal.

Natural elements

Vary the textural elements with other ingredients. Stone is an especially good partner – you could choose a limestone, sandstone or slate floor, for example, or a granite or terrazzo worktop, the latter highly polished to echo the reflectivity of metal. For greater contrast, show off the grain of varnished wood, as cupboard fronts or panelling on walls, or perhaps paint units with a pastel shade of matt emulsion. Accessorise with displays of glassware, clear or frosted, crockery in pretty colours and interesting shapes, and bowls of fruit or vases of flowers for a bright finishing touch.

▶ Old-fashioned tea towels with traditional woven patterns have an enduring appeal.

▶ Elegantly plain glassware looks beautiful displayed on a clear glass shelf.

Farmhouse fresh

CHOOSE CLASSIC DESIGNS TO CREATE A KITCHEN THAT'S HOMELY AND COMFORTABLE. ALONGSIDE BARE WOOD, NEAT PAINTWORK AND CERAMIC TILES, ADD SIMPLE GLASSWARE AND OLD-FASHIONED TEA TOWELS TO CREATE A TIMELESS MIX THAT WILL NEVER LET YOU DOWN.

There's a preponderance of wood in this typical farmhouse-style kitchen, but it's been designed with variety in mind: the old wood of the chest of drawers, which is agreeably marked and worn-in, is contrasted with the new wood of the work surface, necessarily smooth and even. The floor is made from boards of a darker wood, which offset the cornflower-blue units. You could achieve this look with pale floorboards by staining or painting them and, if you like the unsophisticated effect of reclaimed wood, search out old pieces of furniture junk shops, or find a maker who uses reclaimed timber in his or her designs.

Traditional decor

The prettiness of the golden worktops and painted units (low-shine, oil-based eggshell or vinyl silk withstands knocks is complemented by peach-coloured ceramic tiles, which have a gentle sheen and rustic finish completely in keeping with the style of this room. For a slightly more decorative finish, you could choose one-colour embossed tiles, or lay plain tiles at 45 degrees for a diagonal pattern.

The solid, hard surfaces of any kitchen benefit from a contrast with lighter, softer textures. Here, translucent glassware has been displayed on open shelves or in cupboards with glass doors; combining open and enclosed storage allows you to show off attractive objects while keeping clutter hidden away. Or display coloured crockery, wicker baskets, linen towels or wooden bowls to provide a variety of textures and maintain the simple, farmhouse feel.

farmhouse fresh

These materials are designed to work together to evoke a particular atmosphere: rustic, informal, and cozy. Their textures are wonderfully varied, which gives the room extra vitality and charm.

Kitchen textures

CERAMIC TILES
Smooth and glossy, ceramic tiles make a good contrast to rougher textures in a farmhouse-style kitchen. **449**

RIVEN SLATE
Extremely matte and fairly uneven, this hand-split slate would make an extraordinary kitchen floor. **550**

WIRED GLASS
Wired glass instantly conjures up a traditional look and feel. You could use it for cupboard doors, shelves or even a tabletop. **415**

STRIPED WEAVE
Plain, striped, or checked fabrics are an ideal choice for this look. This linen-cotton mix has a stripey textural pattern. **178**

OAK FLOORING
The ultimate in classic flooring, oak boards have a warm, friendly quality, and an attractive texture and pattern. **505**

RAGGED PAINT EFFECT
Rag-rolled paintwork makes a beautiful background for a country-style room. **104**

This kitchen's simple style comes from the panelled design of its units, combined with soft colours, natural wood and hand-made ceramic tiles.

▲ A creamy yellow background works well with the textures of old wood, matt metal, traditional glass, ceramic tableware, slate and a wicker log baske

Sophisticated dining

◀ Use toning paints as an effective backdrop for hard and soft textures, and dramatic contrasts of colour.

FOR AN UNHURRIED BREAKFAST, CASUAL LUNCH OR FRIENDLY SUPPER, DECORATE YOUR DINING ROOM WITH RELAXED, SOFT TONES, LETTING A CAREFUL MIX OF INTERESTING TEXTURES PROVIDE AN ATTRACTIVE AND COMFORTABLE BACKGROUND.

Who says walls should always be the same colour? The great thing about using paint is that it's inexpensive and easy to apply – and so allows you enormous freedom to experiment with unusual styles and textures.

Paint walls in two, three or more complementary shades and, as shown in the funky, informal dining area to the left, the results can be really impressive. What's more, even though the colours are different, the surface gives one subtle, uniform texture against which to play around with a few dashing contrasts. A warm wool carpet, for example, makes a soft and welcoming flooring, although one could just as easily picture in this environment limed-wood floorboards, natural fibre matting or even groovy rubber.

The furniture is equally striking; wood with metal has a look that's both fashionable and functional, and its square shapes play against the circular pattern of the rug, while the dramatic mix of reflective steel and dark, grainy wood is both sleek and modern.

Subtle variety

More classic in style, but nevertheless highly appealing, is the simple dining room on the far left, painted in buttermilk yellow with a scrubbed plank floor. The muted blue (and hard, matt texture) of the slate hearth is a lovely complement, as is the pale lilac of the soft pashmina throw that's been casually hung over the back of a dining chair.

In fact, the varied textures that have been employed to create this room are so sophisticated they take a while to become apparent: frosted plastic and wire for the modern chandelier, for example; opaque muslin blinds; carved-wood salad servers; a chunky, woven-wicker log basket; clear glass wine goblets; shiny, cream-coloured crockery. It's just the sort of delicious, delightful combination that you can enjoy at your leisure over a delicious, relaxing meal with friends or family.

sophisticated dining

Warm, subtle and interesting textures are ideal for a dining room that you wish to be contemporary but not aggressive or difficult to live with. Mix a background of smooth paintwork with exotic woods, soft wool carpet and intriguing fabrics.

Dining room textures

MATT PAINT
Use matt emulsion as a neutral background, but in a pretty colour that complements others in the room.
57

WOOL CARPET
A tufted carpet cut in stripes of two lengths is another way to increase textural interest.
252

EXOTIC WOOD
Rather than choosing a standard wood for furniture or wall panels, you could opt for a stunningly unusual type such as this kevazing veneer.
513

METALLIC SILK
This beautiful fabric is smooth, shiny and extremely elegant. Use it for dining chairs, cushions and drapes.
188

WALLPAPER
Though often patterned, wallpapers can be plain and simple, making an understated textural background.
321

SILK SHEER
A barely-there muslin is a superb ingredient in this type of scheme.
140

Pastel prettiness

WHETHER YOU DECORATE YOUR BATHROOM IN TRADITIONAL OR CONTEMPORARY STYLE, USING A RANGE OF PRETTY CANDY COLOURS WILL ALWAYS ENSURE IT'S A WARM AND WELCOMING HAVEN FOR REFRESHING RELAXATION.

Even with the plainest of fittings you can use colour and texture to give a boring bathroom extra interest, while if you're lucky enough to have a statement-making bath or basin they can help to show it off. Take a painted plaster wa as a starting point. Why not add a few rows of shiny cerami tiles, hand-made so they have a slightly mottled surface and uneven edges – and choose a range of colours that contra nicely but still look good together? Or you could use vinyl rubber tiles for a softer, warmer surface, or simply paint a checkerboard of colour using small tins of gloss paint. Wood-covered walls, either square panels of MDF or made from tongue-and-groove, can also be painted, in squares o stripes, and there's nothing to stop you continuing your design over the floor as well, if you so wish.

Original thinking

It's this type of lateral thinking that makes the difference between bland and beautiful. Storage, for example, is vital as a means of hiding away all those bathroom bits and pieces, but it doesn't have to be the standard, typical types You can adapt home office-style units and keep towels in th larger drawers at the bottom with bottles and lotions at the top; or perhaps use wicker baskets, opaque plastic bins, wood and glass cabinets or shiny metal boxes. Pick styles, colours and textures that work with your overall scheme bu at the same time, don't be afraid to use your imagination an have some fun.

▲ Shiny metal, ceramic tiles and laminate drawer fronts: all hard surfaces, but with subtle textural variety.

▶ Machine-washable cotton bath mats are practical and pleasant to use; the ribbed texture of these examples gives them a nicely three-dimensional quality.

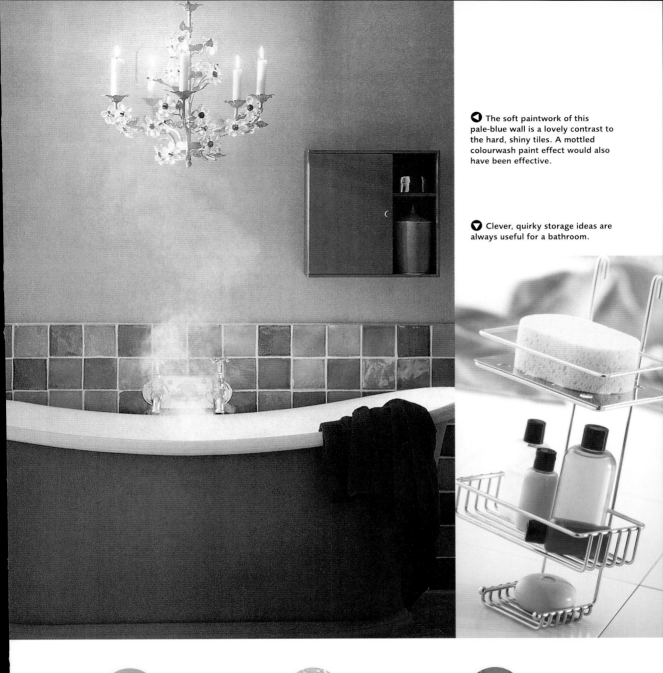

● The soft paintwork of this pale-blue wall is a lovely contrast to the hard, shiny tiles. A mottled colourwash paint effect would also have been effective.

▼ Clever, quirky storage ideas are always useful for a bathroom.

...el prettiness

...ink laterally, even
...hen you're on a
...dget. **Pick a**
...nge of delicious
...bble-gum colours,
...d vary the
...xtural contrasts
...om plastic to
...ass, ceramic to
...lourwashed
...int.

342

Bathroom textures

LINOLEUM FLOORING
This dimpled surface would make a pretty base for an inexpensive bathroom.

354

PVC SHEET
A coloured plastic shower curtain can completely transform even the dullest bathroom.

381

LAMINATE SURFACE
This type of graphic, abstract pattern would offset plain paintwork and sanitary ware.

391

TEXTURED GLASS
For privacy in a bathroom door or window, or for interesting shelves and fittings.

447

CERAMIC TILES
The uneven colouring and surface of the tiles add interest.

106

PAINT EFFECT
Jazz up a boring room with an attractive colourwash paint effect.

swatch

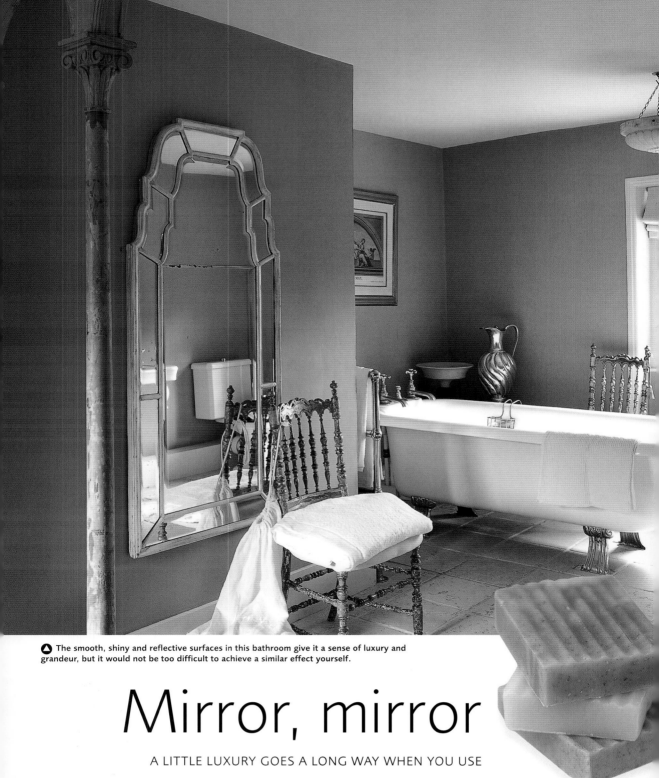

△ The smooth, shiny and reflective surfaces in this bathroom give it a sense of luxury and grandeur, but it would not be too difficult to achieve a similar effect yourself.

Mirror, mirror

A LITTLE LUXURY GOES A LONG WAY WHEN YOU USE
MATERIALS THAT ADD A FEELING OF INDULGENCE TO YOUR
BATHROOM. IT'S NOT NECESSARY TO SPEND LOTS OF MONEY,
AS CLEVER THINKING CAN CREATE IMPRESSIVE EFFECTS.

△ Treat yourself to some expensive soaps and add colour and texture to a bathroom.

mirror, mirror

Certain textures create the effect of opulence and indulgence. Make a lasting impression by selecting the surfaces that are stippled, marbled, gilded and covered in mosaic.

Bathroom textures

METALLIC PAINT Spray metallic paint onto junk-shop furniture and the piece will be transformed. For a distressed look, lightly sand the corners once the paint has dried.

96

STIPPLING Stippled walls offer subtle interest. Let one coat of paint dry, then use a stippling brush, textured roller or marine sponge to break up a second coat (in a contrasting colour) while it's still wet.

98

GLASS MOSAIC Small areas of metallic mosaic tiles give dazzling results. For a less intense yet still interesting look, use plain tiles with metallic ones set at random intervals.

427

MARBLE SLAB Cool, hard and smooth, marble is marvellous in a bathroom. This rose-coloured example is especially pretty.

562

MARBLE BRICKS A more intricate but rather understated effect comes from laying marble as brick-shaped flooring.

576

's all too easy for a modern bathroom to be a flat, lifeless place, but if you can include one or two sumptuous pieces which have glorious texture it will make an enormous difference to the atmosphere.

A fabulous room such as the one on the left, filled with gilding, metal, mirrors and antiques, may not be possible for all of us – but it can still offer some brilliant decorating ideas. The pitted stone floor, for example, looks marvelous against the ultra-smooth, putty-coloured walls. If you can't have one, however, you could substitute reclaimed and limewashed wooden boards, or else use marble-effect linoleum or even imitation-stone vinyl. This will give you a pale (but interesting) base against which everything else in the room will look even more wonderful.

Gorgeous gilding

The huge, cast-iron roll-top bath on the far left is certainly an eye-catching piece, but you can transform the looks of even

the most ordinary bath by simply changing the taps. As for the gorgeous gilded chairs, consider scouring junk shops for an old dining chair or two (they needn't match), then try gilding them yourself, or spray paint them with metallic paint. An uneven result is ideal – both charming and full of texture. Then add other second-hand finds such as wash stands with bowls and jugs, mirrors (the more the merrier and, again, you could spray the frames yourself) and intriguing pictures, plus beautiful accessories, from natural sea sponges to luxurious coloured and scented soaps.

As a finishing touch, how about changing the handles on drawers or cupboard doors? It's simple enough to do – you just need a little ingenuity. You could, for example, replace dull, ordinary ones with interesting textural types such as seashells or pebbles, rope or leather pulls, cut-glass knobs or stainless-steel bars – the only limit is your imagination.

◖ Cool, hard marble is a wonderful bathroom luxury, and looks fabulous next to the soft sheen of brass and the roughness of a natural sponge.

Professional but still personal

MAKE WORKING FROM HOME A PLEASURE RATHER THAN A CHORE BY SURROUNDING YOURSELF WITH FURNITURE AND ACCESSORIES THAT ARE FULL OF CHARACTER, AND USING ONLY COLOURS AND TEXTURES THAT YOU REALLY LOVE.

▲ Details make all the difference, and even a tiny touch such as unusual picture frames will add great textural interest.

If you're of a fairly-laid back disposition, then your desk, like the one shown right, may be the ideal place for an impromptu stack of colourful paperbacks. At least it gives it a casual appearance that belies its workmanlike functions: drawers full of filing, a large, clear surface and a bright, adjustable lamp.

Deliberate disguise

Sometimes the last thing you want your home office to look like is just that – an office. Painting the walls in a muted colour and adding a few favorite objects is the best way to disguise its business-oriented elements. The resulting textural mix will give it a subliminal appeal, too. Even computers these days come in attractive colours, and if you really hate the sight of hi-tech gadgets then you could hide them away, either inside a cupboard (buy one ready-made or ask a carpenter to make a built-in version) or behind a fold-away screen, perhaps made of wood, paper or frosted glass.

If you've got the space, there's no reason why you shouldn't include a well-padded armchair – or even a couc – for those contemplative moments, with cushions in luxurious velvet, mohair or jumbo cord. Sometimes it's good to question the accepted way of doing things, and not all of us work best when sitting in an office chair. Papers could be stored in woven baskets rather than conventional cardboard files; notebooks could be covered leather, suede or hand-made paper; then just add painting small sculptures, pretty ceramics and, as a finishing touc a vase of sweet-smelling flowers.

▲ If you want to create a character office, choose clever storage such as the circular plastic stacking uni

▶ This unconventional home office contains a gentle mix appealing textures, from the natural wood of the desk to chrome and glass lamp, and the leather-covered boo

professional but still personal

A good variety of pleasant textures makes a noticeable difference to the way that a home office feels. Think of it as a domestic rather than a company-style environment, and include only materials that give you great pleasure and enjoyment.

Home office textures

BIRCH FLOORING
Natural, unpainted wood has an enjoyable grain and texture. A type such as this is unpretentious and helps create a comfortable feel.
521

TEXTURED PAPER
Light and delicate, the texture of paper can lift and brighten a room. Use it for informal lampshades and notebooks.
310

JUMBO CORD
Beautiful fabrics help soften a work room, whatever its style. The fabulous stripes of this jumbo cord would also look good in a living room.
210

TUFTED RUG
A patterned rug adds color and interest; its pleasurable cosy texture is another advantage in a home working space.
245

SOFT SUEDE
You'll appreciate a touch of luxury when you're feeling stressed or stretched at work. Suede, leather, and velvet bring that indulgent feel.
224

TEXTURED GLASS
Use textured glass in a fold-away screen to partition your room for privacy, yet still keep a light, airy feel.
406

making a home office work

A combination of colour, texture and pattern can make even the most inexpensive of materials interesting and attractive.

Home office textures

PATTERNED GLASS
Use toughened, textured glass for an unusual, see-through desktop rested on simple trestle legs.

409

SMOOTH PVC
Smooth plastic often has grooved, saturated colour and makes a bright, bold statement.

353

LINOLEUM FLOORING
Inexpensive, durable and easy-to-clean, this flooring features statement-making graphic embossed disks.

345

WOOL CARPET
A neutral-coloured carpet can provide a good base if you're planning to inject spots of colour elsewhere.

254

CHIPBOARD
Although usually painted over, you may prefer chipboard's interesting texture when left bare.

519

Making a
home office work

● Wood, glass and plastic combine for an inexpensive but highly efficient and texturally interesting workspace.

● The roll-top front of this prettily coloured melamine storage cabinet minimises space yet allows easy access to files.

Why make life complicated? A thick sheet of strengthened glass laid securely on two painted or unpainted wood (or metal) trestle legs may be all you need as your home office desk. Not only is it large, stable and level, it's also good-looking and easy to use.

You can then base your scheme around the contrast of glass and metal or glass and wood, adding some open shelving units, chests of drawers or simple individual shelves fixed to the walls. Your chair could, similarly, be made of metal or wood, while a desk lamp might have a wooden base with frosted glass shade, or be in the form of a metal hinged-arm light. If you wish, consider adding another texture with either matt or shiny plastic: it's both practical and inexpensive for chairs, lights, or storage units and accessories such as fans, pen holders and filing trays, and comes in a wide variety of pretty colours.

Trade tips

The simplest treatment for walls is to paint them a muted, matt background colour – though shiny gloss paint would be extra hard-wearing as an alternative. Or you could use blackboard paint – ideal for a home office or a child's room – on which you could write and wipe messages and memos. A fantastically useful and visually interesting addition would be to screw a large steel sheet to the wall to act as a magnetic notice board. And a cheap finishing touch would be magazine files made of cardboard. If you're really short of money, there's nothing wrong with using old shoe boxes (cover them in wrapping paper if you want a more finished effect) or painted fruit crates as an unusual means of storage.

● A whimsical plastic floor fan adds an element of fun to working from home.

SETTING UP A HOME OFFICE CAN SOMETIMES BE AN EXPENSIVE BUSINESS – BUT IT DOESN'T HAVE TO BE SO. IF YOU CHOOSE YOUR FURNISHINGS CAREFULLY THEY CAN BE BOTH FUNCTIONAL AND ATTRACTIVE, WITHOUT COSTING A FORTUNE.

Strong

BOLD, **BRIGHT** COLOURS ARE INVIGORATING, **DRAMATIC** AND SOPHISTICATED. THEY MAKE A **SUPERB** PARTNER FOR TEXTURES WITH **CHARACTER**, RESULTING IN ROOMS THAT NEVER FAIL TO **IMPRESS**.

colours

STRONG COLOURS

Within a
ur scheme
ed around a
ne of watery
s, the owner
his bathroom
also
mbled
ever range of
t and shiny,
gh and
oth textures.

Bold,
ptural shapes
really
hasise a
natic colour
eme, as shown
his modern
g room.

Any decorating scheme that uses strong colours is bound to make a big impression. However eye-catching strong colours are, though, they don't have to be brash or unpleasantly bright – clever thinking can create rooms that are interesting and involving without being horribly over the top.

Many people think of bold colours as being just the three primaries: red, yellow and blue. Splashes of these can look fantastic (think of Chinese red lacquered boxes or brilliant blue glass), but when used over large areas they are best suited to a children's bedroom or playroom. Consider, instead, other strong colours that will appear more sophisticated: they work well in families, such as aubergine, claret, midnight blue and bottle green; spicy tones such as red ochre, mustard, cinnamon and saffron; or Mediterranean shades such as sea blue, yellow or aquamarine.

Start by just using one bold colour, perhaps surrounded by neutrals, and if you're feeling daring add one or two others in a complementary shade. Be careful with contrasts – small doses are best, or you'll end up with a busy, clamourous room in which every colour is competing for attention.

Strong colour schemes are more versatile than you might think. They can often, for example, create a wonderful ethnic or global style, with the use of dyed raffia, tin ornaments, sheer or opaque fabrics (perhaps with a metallic weave), paper wall hangings and woven rugs. Or, when used with appropriate furnishings, they can suggest a historical style such as Georgian, Victorian or even '50s or '60s. And they can be highly contemporary, incorporating funky, fun textures from rubber and plastic to coloured acrylic and fibre-optic fabrics.

Perhaps the most important thing to bear in mind when using bold colours is that they shouldn't overpower the textures you have chosen. Get the best from strong colours by treating them in a measured, thoughtful way, and they will enhance a textural scheme to truly stunning effect.

VIVID, SPICY REDS ARE REMINISCENT OF
AFRICA AND INDIA – USE WARM WOOL AND SOFT
COTTON TO OFFSET THE GLAMOROUS SHIMMER OF
SILK FOR A SUMPTUOUS AND DRAMATIC SCENE.

Global influence

◐ A three-dimensional pile is a subtle touch on a searingly bright tufted rug: it would be best used in a fairly large, uncluttered room alongside a few bold ethnic accessories.

◐ The accessories in this room – a clear ass vase, white ceramic bowl and asketware plant holder – have been ept quite plain so as not to detract from e vitality of the fabrics.

Instead of using paint, why not cover wall with a hanging made from expensive fabric, or even paper? e textural effect, as shown here, amazing.

Eastern-style piles of floor cushions make a modern statement in a living room, and are a great way to create textural contrast – you can use as many different fabrics as you like, simply linking them by colour, shape and graduating size. Even if you're on a budget, you might be able to find small remnants of expensive or unusual fabric which will lift your scheme no end.

You can vary the look by adding all sorts of fabulous trimmings: ribbon, beading, raffia, sequins, rows of buttons, ric-rac, even feathers. Each cushion can be made from two or more types of material: go for the ultimate in contrast with, say, linen next to velvet, organza layered over satin, or perhaps sari fabric with plain cotton. The same goes for drapes, too. The main picture shows how thick, heavy wool drapes have been given a quirky, scalloped trim. An edging made of velvet or linen would have been equally attractive, or perhaps a deep border along the bottom in vibrant red felt.

Ethnic accents

As much as fabrics, your choice of accessories will help shape the style of the room, whether they be oriental red lacquer boxes, embossed brass trays from India or painted African gourds. If you want to keep the look fairly low-key, however, stick to furniture, walls and floors in plain, subtle shapes and materials. In this contemporary room, for example, white walls and a relatively plain white couch have been teamed with a simple metal and marble coffee table and a natural wool carpet, creating a neutral background that allows touches of bold colour and texture to be seen at their best.

global influence

Choose a selection of sumptuous fabrics and balance them with plainer materials such as leather, wood and glass.

Living room textures

CRACKLED PAINT EFFECT
Dramatic on a wall, this paint effect could be used on accessories such as wooden picture frames or lamp bases.
113

CHENILLE VELVET
Uneven brushing on the soft pile of this tawny-coloured velvet gives it a fascinating, luxurious texture.
202

FAKE LEATHER
Hide – whether genuine or fake – adds an upmarket look. This example would make a marvellous cover for a large floor cushion.
221

NEEDLEPOINT RUG
The stitched surface of a needlepoint rug is a good alternative to the fluffier texture of a cut-pile version.
249

WOVEN LEATHER
Weaving leather strips results in a fabulously chunky surface and makes attractive contemporary cushions and other accessories.
296

swatch

Moody blues

A DARING USE OF ONE STRONG COLOUR CAN HAVE
ENORMOUS IMPACT – IT LOOKS ESPECIALLY GOOD
WHEN MIXED WITH THE NATURAL BEAUTY OF GRAINY
WOOD, RUGGED STONE AND HAIRY COIR.

One way to approach a living room scheme is by thinking of it in terms of layers. Start with the floor – to create the look of a room like the one on the right, place a large natural fibre mat (coir, seagrass, sisal or rush) over a stone floor. These tiles are made of terracotta, but limestone, sandstone or perhaps even concrete slabs would work equally well.

The contrast of these two textures is a good way to begin and can be built upon with the wall treatment – perhaps smooth paintwork, as here, or a rougher plaster finish, or maybe paper-backed hessian for an earthy, rustic effect. This room has the advantage of an interesting ceiling, too. If you're lucky enough to have exposed wooden beams, you could leave them bare, stain them or paint them to match your color scheme.

Finishing touches

Window treatments add another layer. Here, a simple approach has been taken, with unbleached linen in informal gathers and tied back with an oversized woven tassel – it's an echo of the rough-and-smooth floor treatment and is both easy and inexpensive to achieve. Furniture and accessories are your final layer. Large pieces made from sustainable tropical hardwood look good in this room, though old pine would be just as attractive, as would a combination of stone and metal. The couch and chairs manage to be both smart and comfortable, and a few pieces of glassware in toning colours complete the look superbly.

▲ A chenille-covered couch offers subtle textural interest, especially when teamed with cushions trimmed with piping. A mohair or felt throw would add a soft touch.

---

moody blues

With strong colours, a balanced mix of textures is vital. Combine hard and soft, rough and smooth, hairy and silky, opaque and sheer, to result in a room that has unquestionable appeal

Living room textures

315 HESSIAN WALLCOVERING
This has a subtle texture that would complement both rough and smooth surfaces.

153 TEXTURED SHEER
An unusual fabric that adds interest when used for blinds or other soft furnishings.

413 PATTERNED GLASS
Use for a coffee table top, a cupboard door or an uplit shelf.

TERRACOTTA FLOOR TILE
Old terracotta floor tiles have a delightful patina that makes an excellent base for a room. Top with a rug for softness.

SMOOTH COTTON
Workmanlike cotton is inexpensive, easy to clean, and long-lasting.

SISAL/FLAX FLOORING
This flooring is relatively neutral, but has a subtle texture

▼ Candles in interesting colours are an attractive accessory, even when unlit.

◄ The textural scheme has been built up layer by layer in this airy room for a relaxing balance of hard and soft, rough and smooth, clear and opaque.

flame shades

Don't compete with bold colours by using too many surfaces. Variety is good, but choose calm, smooth textures like oak, leather and glass.

Living room textures

SANDBLASTED GLASS
Glass can be smooth and matt, or highly polished, with unusual patterns and contrasts of opacity and clarity.

401

SMOOTH COTTON
Smooth cotton is practical and useful – it will complement almost every other material without detracting from them.

171

TEXTURED CHENILLE
The warm, inviting texture of chenille is soft and giving, making a pleasant change from harder, colder surfaces.

205

PIERCED LEATHER
Leather, though sophisticated, is fairly unobtrusive, and will work well in any type of room scheme.

227

OAK FLOORBOARDS
The satiny, shiny surface of oak, with its beautiful grained pattern, makes an excellent choice for an upmarket and attractive floor.

499

LIMESTONE SLAB
While limestone is essentially cold and smooth, its slightly rough surface is full of character and perfectly complements the softer textures of fabric.

528

Flame shades

WARM, VIBRANT AND WELCOMING, SPLASHES OF BRILLIANT RED OR ORANGE ADD A TOUCH OF DRAMA TO A LIVING ROOM COMBINE WITH RELAXED NEUTRALS AND THE RESULT IS A SCHEME THAT'S INSTANTLY UPLIFTING

▼ An unconventional colour combines with an unusual texture to make this seating unique and eye-catching

◀ Silk in shades from tangerine to magenta makes ideal scatter cushions or even imposing curtains.

◀ This rug makes a dramatic centrepiece to a room which is otherwise filled with the neutral colours and natural textures of leather, stone, brick, metal and wood.

When attempting a dramatic colour scheme, it's best to do a fair amount of research and preparation first. Tear pages out of magazines, brush sample pots of paint onto walls and pin fabric swatches together, until you've got a clear feel for what you're doing. Allow one colour to dominate, perhaps using others as accents. Or, for a more low-key look, team just one strongly coloured piece (a rug, couch or painting, for example) with surroundings in beautiful neutrals.

Colourful effects

Creating an eye-catching living room, for example, is easy if you choose seating in brilliant colours such as the orange couches and chairs shown on the bottom left. The key is to let such a vivid colour make its impact without distraction, by keeping everything else in the room subtle and undemanding. Here, walls are plain white and the floor a simple wood that has a gentle sheen, while the glass coffee table and slender metal and plastic lamp are so understated as to be almost invisible. What's more, all these smooth, hard surfaces make an effective textural contrast to the unusual ruched effect of the fabric seat covers.

In a cosy sitting room like the one on the top left, a red, yellow and black rug becomes the focal point in front of a glowing fire. Its tufted surface happily combines with the other textures in the room – smooth leather, pitted stone, rough metal, crunchy linen and grained wood – and its inviting colour demonstrates how these shades can be used successfully in settings that range from the ultra-modern to the typically traditional.

◀ A plastic chair in tomato red could be used for occasional seating or in a home office. Wherever it's placed, it will certainly make a statement.

All-out glamour

WHEN YOU WANT TO GIVE THAT BOUDOIR
FEEL TO A BEDROOM, COMBINE VIBRANT SHADES
OF PINK AND RED WITH THE LUXURIOUS TEXTURES
OF SILK AND VELVET, THROWING IN TASSELS,
GILT AND QUILTING FOR ADDED IMPACT.

However much you love strong colours, they're not always
the most restful choice for a bedroom – though they can
work wonderfully as vivid accents in a room that's otherwise
fairly neutral. On the right, for example, a sky-blue quilted
eiderdown with vivid pink flowers makes a dramatic focal
point for a bed that's covered in cool, calm ivory and oyster
coloured fabrics. The fabulous texture of quilted silk subtly
links the bold and the understated shades, while in the
background the intricate carving of the oversized wooden
door is nicely complementary; it also provides a hard, rough
texture to counterpoint the luxurious softness everywhere
else in the room.

Impressive ingenuity

This effect can be emulated relatively easily, by choosing
plain white or off-white bed linen and simply adding a
brightly coloured eiderdown, bedcover or throw in suitably
luxurious fabric: perhaps silk satin, like in this opulent room,
or else mohair, cashmere, soft wool, velvet or even
pashmina. If your budget won't stretch to brand-new, ready-
made textiles, look for discounted ends of lines or remnants,
or check out second-hand shops or jumble sales for pieces
that could be washed, cut up and adapted – you may only
need a smallish square to make a central panel around which
you could sew a plain border.

These smooth, soft textures can be nicely contrasted
with a bare wooden floor, roughly plastered walls or carved
wooden mirrors or picture frames. A lamp with a branch-
like wooden base – as seen in the bedroom above left –
some pieces of hand-thrown pottery or a couple of woven
storage baskets would all be ideal additions to this look. Or
if you want a more feminine, film-star style, choose pieces
such as the Parisian-style metal chair below right, with its
plush upholstery and tasseled fringe. Alternatively, you
could add gilded picture frames, antique engraved glass
goblets, assorted candle-holders and maybe even an
eccentric lampshade made of plastic, taffeta or feathers.

▶ **This pretty bedroom contrasts
rough and smooth, sheer and
opaque, hard and soft. The pink
is saved from being overpowering
by the plentiful use of white.**

swatch

all-out glamour

**These textures have been chosen for their no-holds-barred,
glamorous effect: linen, chenille, taffeta, a tufted sheer and an
exotic zebra-skin print. Ensure, however, that you give soft fabrics a
counterpoint by using harder surfaces as well.**

Bedroom textures

ROUGH PLASTER
Offset luxurious fabrics with
a few harder, rougher
surfaces such as this unevenly
applied plaster.
481

NATURAL LINEN
Crisp and clean, with a
noticeable weave, pure
linen is unmistakably smart
and elegant.
185

FAKE ZEBRA SKIN
Place a dramatic fake zebra
skin on the floor or over a
bed as the focal point of a
boudoir-style bedroom.
230

CRUNCHY TAFFETA
Delicate and pretty taffeta
is an ideal choice when
you're aiming for a highly
feminine room scheme.
218

SOFT CHENILLE
This gorgeously soft, unevenly
woven texture complements
the fabric's deeply saturated
raspberry pink colour.
204

TUFTED COTTON SHEER
These soft bobbles add
fun and interest to what
could otherwise be a fairly
uninteresting fabric.
144

The opulent effect of quilting on a silk-
 fabric is emphasised by the use of a
 splash of colour and also by the rough
dness of the wooden door.

This junk-shop chair with its raffish
elegance and air of '50s Paris would
add plenty of character to a
boudoir-style bedroom.

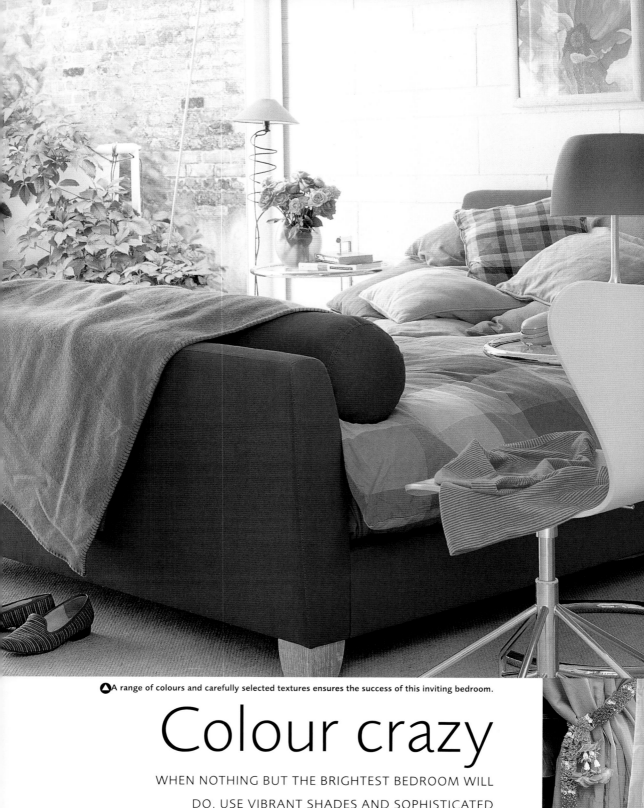

▲A range of colours and carefully selected textures ensures the success of this inviting bedroom.

Colour crazy

WHEN NOTHING BUT THE BRIGHTEST BEDROOM WILL
DO, USE VIBRANT SHADES AND SOPHISTICATED
TEXTURES TO CREATE A TRULY DRAMATIC IMPACT.

nish designer Verner Panton once said that one sits more
mfortably on a colour that one likes. The same could be
d for sleeping, bathing, eating, working…. In fact, if you
oy colour there's no reason why you shouldn't have fun
ng it throughout your home.

ild at heart

create an exuberant, appealing colour mix, start by
oosing a theme – which may be just one colour range or a
nbination of shades that work well together – and ensure
t your textural contrasts are fairly subtle: too much
ture as well as colour could be over-the-top. In the light-
d bedroom on the left, the colours chosen are very
ed – lime green, pink, cornflower blue, lilac, orange and
ow – but all have a similar depth of tone (there are no
tels or dark shades) and a lovely Mediterranean-style
hness. What's more, they're limited to the bed frame,
linen, chair and lamps, all of which have a plain, smooth
ure. The floor has been chosen for its neutral colour and
ure; the main surface interest is the rough, uneven
, painted a contrasting bright white to offset the
m's contents.

n the vivid pink bedroom on the right, by comparison,
colours are less varied and the textures more so: smooth
ted wood and walls have been teamed with soft, frilly
, hard, shiny glass and the feathery trim of the coat
ging beside the bed. Not everyone would welcome such
nsity of colour, but it does work, thanks to a thoughtful
of texture and a willingness to be a little different.

A plastic tie-back is an unusual choice, but here it perfectly
plements the bold colours of the drapes themselves.

▲ There's a definite sense of theatricality to this room; the intensity of the hot pink is
offset by an enjoyable variety of textures.

Bedroom textures

154 **LAYERED SHEER**
Three layers of light, sheer
polyester in various colours –
perfect for an unusual blind.

LACE
Old-fashioned lace is a
wonderful addition to
bedroom, whether the look
is classic or more eclectic

347 **LINOLEUM FLOORING**
An unusual idea for a
bedroom, you could also use
lino with a textured pattern.

 COLOURED GLASS
A smooth, matt, coloured
glass would look calm and
quiet in a bedroom with
plenty of colour and texture

362 **ACRYLIC SHEETING**
Intensely coloured
smooth plastic with a
laid-back texture.

 LAMBSKIN
Indulge yourself with a
furry rug or throw – it's
three-dimensional and
very tactile

swatch

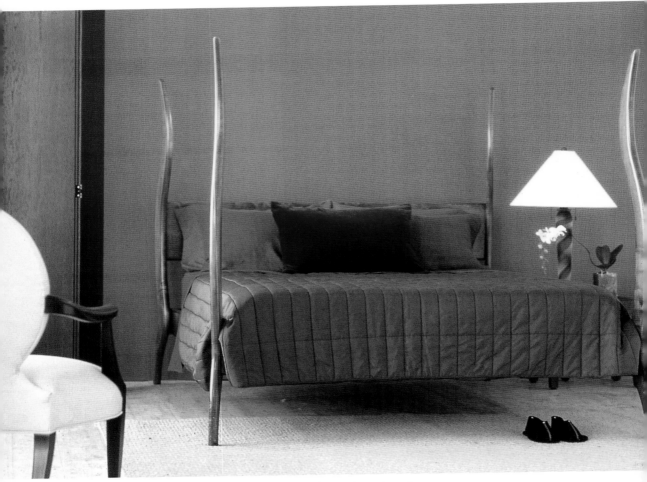

▲ A combination of simple textures is all that's needed when using such a striking colour scheme.

Simple intensity

THE BOLD TONES OF SCARLET, CRIMSON, MAUVE AND PURPLE INDICATE INTIMACY, LUXURY AND OPULENCE. REALLY VIVID COLOURS SUCH AS THESE CAN SUCCEED IN A BEDROOM IF YOU HAVE THE CONFIDENCE TO TAKE A NO-HOLDS-BARRED APPROACH.

When making a daring statement, it's generally best to choose relatively uncomplicated textures. The smooth w in the room above, for example, is offset by a lovely roug coir floorcovering in an unusual pale colour, and the fabr on the bed are straightforward linen, velvet and quilted nylon, with no fancy borders, trims, buttons or tassels. E piece in the room has a simple, graphic quality, and that extends particularly to the furniture, which demonstrates strong, pared-down shapes and clean lines – it makes a

A screen is a useful addition to a bedroom; here, it's covered in a soft, warm fabric which contrasts nicely with the stone floor, while mirroring the armchair and silky cushions.

An assortment of strong colours makes this inexpensive bed linen stand out in a stylish statement against the pale walls.

quiet but effective statement that's ideal in this scheme. It's best, after that, to select just a couple of additional colours around which to base your design, either from the same 'family', or to create an unexpected contrast. (How about khaki with scarlet, bottle green with brilliant orange, or navy with lemon yellow? Experiment with fabric swatches and sample paints before committing yourself.) The alternative is to paint walls white and say it all with coloured bed linen: a versatile solution, especially if you buy a variety of sets and mix them to provide an interesting rainbow of colours.

Brilliant brushwork

For the utmost impact with minimum effort and expense, take the simple option of painting just one wall of a bedroom in a vital, intense colour. Matt emulsion will have softness and depth, while gloss will look more sophisticated; or you could try an unusual paint such as suede-effect, pearlescent or even glitter. Choose your shade carefully; it must be one you can live with, and with which you can coordinate bed linen, furniture and accessories without too much difficulty.

simple intensity

Strong but straightforward textures make a clear statement. Team them with a range of bold, contrasting colours and furniture that's been chosen for its graphically pared-down shape.

Bedroom textures

RAG RUG
This modern take on the traditional rag rug has a gorgeous soft, fluffy texture and would be ideal beside a bed.
248

JUMBO CORD
Softly ribbed jumbo cord is perfect for upholstering a bedside chair, or even making a cosy throw or cushion cover.
209

CHERRY WOOD
The deep colour and very definite grain of cherry wood gives it a vital and luxurious appearance.
510

METALLIC SILK
The delicate, shiny surface of this light silk has been shot through with metallic threads, giving it a texture that's subtle yet interesting.
189

▶ Bedroom lighting often has great decorative appeal and can be used to reinforce or contrast with a textural theme.

IT CAN BE HARD TO FIND THE RIGHT SCHEME FOR A TEENAGER'S ROOM, BUT A MIX OF STRONG SHADES IS A GOOD START. THEN PICK INEXPENSIVE, INFORMAL FURNISHINGS AND A RANGE OF APPEALING ACCESSORIES FOR A LOOK THAT'S BOTH TRENDY AND ACHIEVABLE.

Young and fun

swatch

young and fun

Use textures that have strong definition for a confident scheme. Their contrasting surfaces will contribute to the effect when used with a range of complementary colours.

Bedroom textures

KNITTING
Knitted cushion covers or throws are easy to make yourself: if you can't knit, chop up an old sweater, and seam it together.
123

COTTON SHEER
A gauzy window hanging is pretty and practical, allowing light to filter through while also retaining privacy.
143

SHEEPSKIN
The long, three-dimensional pile of fluffy sheepskin is incredibly soft and tactile. It works extremely well on top of wooden floorboards.
237

PATTERNED GLASS
Glass like this adds interest to an exterior window, or could be used equally well for a wardrobe door.
411

WOOL CARPET
This carpet has the look of a natural fibre flooring, but is in fact made of softer wool, so would be ideal in a bedroom.
267

ROUGH PLASTER
A textured-plaster wall finish provides a dramatic background to a bedroom, with other textures being kept relatively plain.
488

In a bedroom based around bold colours, a few statement-making pieces will really pull the look together. It could be bed linen or cushions, a radio or a light, or maybe some special storage boxes. In this bright bedroom, for instance, lemon yellow is offset against two shades of pink to create an eye-catching colour scheme. Just as important, however, is the pleasant range of textures, which are easy-going and also interesting.

It all starts with the wooden floorboards, which have been given a wash with thinned-down paint so that the grain still shows through – the result being more 'finished' than bare boards but still natural in appearance. The timber theme continues with a slatted futon bed base and folding side table, both unpainted and unpretentious; together, however, these elements provide the basics for an attractive scheme that could be emulated quickly, easily and cheaply.

Making an impact

The real scene-stealers in the room, though, are the duvet and cushion covers, in an unmissable range of pretty pinks and a gorgeous variety of textures. The duvet cover has been appliquéd with daisies – a lovely way to jazz up a plain piece of fabric – and the knitted cushions are finished with bobbled, waffle and appliquéd surfaces, themselves a contrast to the smooth knitted throw that's been laid neatly over the end of the bed. The sheer muslin curtain adds another textural layer, while the whole room is completed with the scattering of a few fashionable accessories made from rough, hairy sisal, and smooth, shiny glass and plastic.

nstantly update a plain room by using
ht bed linen and painting spacious boxes
omplementary shades.

⬥ The colours of this pretty room are what
first make an impression, but its textures
have been well thought through, too.

DARK WOOD AND GLEAMING METAL MAKE STUNNING
PARTNERS. THESE ROOMS ARE BASED AROUND AN INTERESTING
JUXTAPOSITION OF HARD TEXTURES AND STRONG COLOURS.

Dark and dramatic

This roughly plastered wall makes a fabulous background to the smoothness of the storage unit – it's a nice way to tone down the sometimes stark feel of a modern kitchen.

dark and dramatic

The hard surfaces of a kitchen provide an ideal opportunity to experiment with interesting textures, colours and patterns.

Kitchen textures

LAMINATE WORK SURFACE
This mysterious, metallic pattern would add vitality even to a relatively plain kitchen.
371

LINOLEUM FLOORING
Lino can imitate various other materials, including aluminium treadplate. Excellent for a kitchen with vigour and verve.
348

GLASS MOSAIC
These sleek mosaic tiles are dazzling in their variety. Their metallic colours and subtly different textures are unusual and eye-catching.
426

MAHOGANY
Very dark woods are fabulous teamed with shiny metal – the combination of their colours and textures gives a glamorous, modern look.
495

An unusual, dark wood makes a dramatic impact in a small kitchen: the example on the left uses walnut, although other exotic yet sustainable types would also be suitable. Plain and simple, the large expanses of cupboard doors are nicely contrasted with a parquet floor made from antique oak, its surface scratched, dented and marked. Completing the picture is a counter top also made from dark wood.

If you have wall units, it's a good idea to hang fluorescent strips beneath them to light your working areas, hiding their glare with a baffle (thin strip of wood) in front. A large panel of stainless steel will help to magnify light, and in this kitchen, reflective metal makes a secondary theme, from the splashback and the extractor hood to the elongated door handles and the bar stools. The final theme is one of glass: at the base of the extractor and in the rows of highly practical storage jars.

The unfitted kitchen

As an alternative to a fully fitted room you could choose several free-standing storage-cum-preparation units. A wooden butcher's block evokes a traditional style, while contemporary, streamlined designs are reminiscent of European homes. Look for details such as wheels or interesting handles, and use the flexibility that this type of kitchen gives you to make the most of other features in your scheme – perhaps a special wall finish, a table lamp or a treasured piece of art or craft.

Modern cutlery and a sculptural glass bowl have a fresh, striking look – perfect with bold colours, metal and exotic woods.

Strong horizontal and vertical lines in this kitchen are emphasised by the long handles on the wooden units. The whole scheme has been carefully thought through and looks ultra-sophisticated.

99

▶ The bold orange of these plastic chairs is nicely offset by pale pine and shiny metal.

▼ Glass has great potential, as the dimpled surface of this table demonstrates.

Making an impact

PICK ONE VIBRANT COLOUR FOR YOUR KITCHEN OR DINING AREA AN

ADD DASHES OF COMPLEMENTARY SHADES. THIS NO-HOLDS-BARRE

APPROACH IS SPIRITED, CHEERFUL AND UPLIFTING TO LIVE WIT

making an impact

Using simple, relatively plain textures is a good idea when your aim is to complement a strong colour scheme. Ensure that they're interesting without being distracting or interfering.

Kitchen textures

79 MATT EMULSION
Kitchen cupboards made of cheap wood can be transformed by bright paint.

410 DIMPLED GLASS
Though clear and relatively unobtrusive, this glass makes a strong impression.

387 LAMINATE SURFACE
A man-made surface can also look good and is cheaper than stone.

538 PINK GRANITE
Granite makes a marvellous kitchen work surface – cool, hard and very distinctive in appearance.

526 LIMESTONE SLAB
A stone floor, such as this limestone slab, will last forever. It's subtle and sophisticated, though not cheap.

514 TROPICAL HARDWOOD
Wood has a gentler, warmer texture than that of stone or glass.

In a kitchen that's dominated by one bold colour, it's really important to get the other elements right. Floors, walls and worksurfaces in natural shades are often the best choice (the floor of the kitchen shown below, for example, is made of honed limestone and the worktop is highly polished pink granite), though sometimes picking out a complementary or contrasting colour will work – with small insets in patterned lino, for example, or the border to a tiled splashback. Here a white wall, covered in matt emulsion, echoes the matt surface of the painted unit doors; it's the different degrees of matt and lustre that add enormous, though subtle, interest to this room.

On the shelf

The centrepiece of this kitchen is the impressive stainless-steel cooker and its extractor hood, flanked by two wall cupboards with doors made of glass and steel. Not only do the latter pull the look together, they also allow an intriguing glimpse of all the bright kitchen bits that have been stored inside. These days, cooking gadgets come in all sorts of glorious colours, so it's possible to transform even the dullest of kitchens with an inexpensive new kettle, juice maker, food processor or whisk.

The same is true of dining areas, too: a neutral table – perhaps made of glass and metal, inexpensive pine or a classic, dark hardwood – makes a versatile centrepiece for chairs in any colour or material you like, whether they be upholstered in velvet or canvas, made from plastic and metal, or in bare or painted wood. Add a table runner, some plants or flowers, mats, crockery, napkins and glasses, in one bold colour or varying candy colours, and you'll easily create a characterful, irresistible setting.

This kitchen has plenty of colour and quite a lot on display: note how the large floor slabs provide a clean, uncomplicated base for this look.

Over the rainbow

WITH A LITTLE COURAGE AND A DASH OF PANACHE, YOU CAN USE STRONG
COLOURS TO CREATE AN EXCITING – AND INEXPENSIVE – SCHEME.

In the background of the dining room on the far left, the living room wall was created by mixing purple pigment with the plaster, then coating with yacht varnish when it was dry.

◀ The simple, straightforward materials used in this room offer a range of attractive textures that pleasantly offset the bold lilac of the wall.

Painting walls, ceiling and woodwork in vibrant colours is a cheap, quick and easy way to transform the character of a room. Bold tones can work particularly well in a dining area, where you want to create an atmosphere of friendliness, vibrancy and expectation that's conducive to enjoyable meals. If you've decided to take the plunge and mix more than one shade, think carefully about which colours will work together. Look at those that come from a similar family – cool, warm, spicy pastels or primaries, for example – and if in doubt be inspired by the graduated shades used in the paint charts at any good hardware store. For extra textural effect, vary the finish from matt to satin to gloss; even with a restricted colour palette this will make a great deal of difference.

When choosing fabrics, pick out one or two of your paint colours or use a limited range of neutrals with a down-to-earth feel such as white muslin, unbleached linen or artist's canvas; there does come a point when too much colour is overwhelming, and simple, soft textures can help tone everything down.

A calming influence

Always try to maintain a balance: strongly coloured or textured areas need to be mitigated by others that are plainer and easier to live with. In these dining areas, for example, while strong tones predominate, the floors and tables are made of plain, unpretentious materials, and the overall effect owes a lot to the light and airy nature of each of the rooms. Accessories have been kept to a minimum and carefully co-ordinated in limited colours – though the owner of the dining room on the far left loves bold colours so much that she couldn't resist adding a set of plastic dining chairs in a variety of pretty shades.

over the rainbow

When you're using several strong shades in one room, ensure that textures are varied but also balanced. Too many funky or dramatic surfaces will only clamour for attention and clash unpleasantly.

Dining room textures

CANVAS FABRIC
Tough canvas fabric is versatile and durable. Its quiet texture will offset more glamorous surfaces.
214

MOTTLED WALLPAPER
Marbled wallpaper makes an interesting background without being overly dramatic.
333

THICK FELT
Warm, fuzzy felt is a pleasant fabric for an informal dining room and comes in an impressive variety of bold colours.
316

CHESTNUT WOOD
The natural patina and soft sheen of wood makes a calming contribution to a scheme such as this.
500

swatch

blue heaven

Use layers of texture to complement strong colours, from linoleum on the floor to wallpaper, unusual paint effects and mosaic tiles.

Bathroom textures

RUBBER MAT
Dimpled rubber has a three-dimensional texture for good grip and an appealing look – great for colourful bath mats.
344

GLASS MOSAIC
Tiny mosaic tiles come in gorgeous saturated colours. Some have a pleasantly uneven, hand-finished texture, as here.
431

PAINT EFFECT
This paint effect only needs a plain white suite and minimal accessories to be the basis for an inspiring bathroom.
118

LINOLEUM FLOORING
As a base for a characterful, colourful room, this textured lino would be hard to beat.
349

CORK FLOOR TILE
Warm and soft underfoot, yet tough and waterproof, cork makes an excellent textured bathroom flooring.
303

TEXTURED WALLPAPER
A subtly textured wallpaper can form an excellent background to bold colours and more noticeable surfaces.
323

▲ An interesting bathroom can easily be created with little expense but a certain amount of ingenuity. H a variety of textures and bold use of colour give the room strong character.

◀ **Mosaic creates a splash of vivid colour and three-dimensional texture. It's not even very difficult to make yourself.**

Bathroom furniture often tends to be straightforward and simple, especially when it's of the less expensive type. You can, however, create a beautifully designed and well-thought-through room based around even the plainest of plain white suites.

Inexpensive ideas

Start by considering either the walls or the floor. The cheapest and easiest option is to paint the walls a wonderful, strong colour – blue or green always looks good in a bathroom, though you may prefer to choose something different – and then lay a water-resistant flooring in either a complementary or a neutral shade.

Bearing in mind the textures of your walls and floor, you can now start to build up other areas of the room bit by bit. Tiny mosaic tiles help to break up expanses of hard, smooth surfaces, and lend themselves well to areas of intense colour. If you can't afford to cover a whole wall in them, you could easily (as shown in the bright bathroom opposite) create a small basin splashback, or perhaps a mirror surround, or a picture frame.

Another choice for frames, or maybe a medicine cabinet, would be plain wood, perhaps with a limed or distressed paint finish. Other storage might consist of glass shelves (good for creating an illusion of lightness and space) and plastic baskets, in bright colours that suit those of the walls and floor. Each of these elements provides another pleasurable texture, while towels, which offer a welcoming soft and fluffy contrast, can be hung from rails or hoops, or stored folded or rolled in shelves, boxes or baskets. And, as a finishing touch, add some houseplants, coloured rubber mats and plastic or glass bottles containing your favorite lotions and potions.

Blue heaven

TAKE A GORGEOUS WASH OF COLOUR AS YOUR BATHROOM STARTING POINT, ADDING ACCESSORIES IN COMPLEMENTARY SHADES AND INTERESTING TEXTURES. PUT IT TOGETHER LAYER BY LAYER AND THE RESULT WILL BE A ROOM WITH PERSONALITY AND PANACHE.

◀ **Dimpled rubber adds a pleasant texture and colour, and is ideal for bath mats.**

Bathing beauties

BATHROOM FURNITURE IN CLEAN, STRUCTURAL SHAPES AND SIMPLE LINES WORKS WELL WITH BOLD COLOURS, WHETHER THE OVERALL STYLE IS CLASSIC, CONTEMPORARY OR A MIXTURE OF THE TWO.

There's a certain timeless elegance to reclaimed stone flags that makes them the perfect choice as a flooring for both traditional and modern bathrooms. They're a great complement to the smoothness of the other elements of the room, maybe because they're slightly rough around the edges. And if you find the idea of stepping out of the bath onto a stone floor a little chilling, there's always the option underfloor heating.

Painted wooden floorboards are a less expensive alternative to a stone floor – several layers of floor paint covered with marine varnish should make them suitably waterproof. Contrast with a wall painted in a definite colour with a solid finish or perhaps colourwashed, dragged or stippled. You could clad the wall in an interesting material tongue-and-groove timber and ceramic tiles are both traditional, but you could also use tiny mosaic tiles, panels of painted and varnished MDF, or wall tiles made of marble or slate.

For further textural impact, there's a wealth of different materials available: baths could be a cast-iron roll-top version, enamelled pressed steel, acrylic or even stainless steel, while basins could be made of glass, stone or wood instead of the conventional ceramic. That's not to mention unfitted pieces and accessories where there are, of course, endless possibilities.

A lasting impression

The key to a successful bathroom of this type, however, is your choice of furniture, both fitted and free-standing. Think of shapes that are clean and simple, and individual pieces that make an impact. Select strong lines and don't clutter room. Whether you select renovated antiques or fashionable new designs, what's important is that the scheme makes a big impression with the least amount of fuss.

▲ **A fabulous combination of textures: diamond-sawn slate wall tiles, a wood, chrome and glass basin, and thickly ribbed towels.**

◄ **An antique French chair is partly decorative, partly functional in the corner of a bathroom. Its worn metal works well with the roughly painted wall and reclaimed stone flags.**

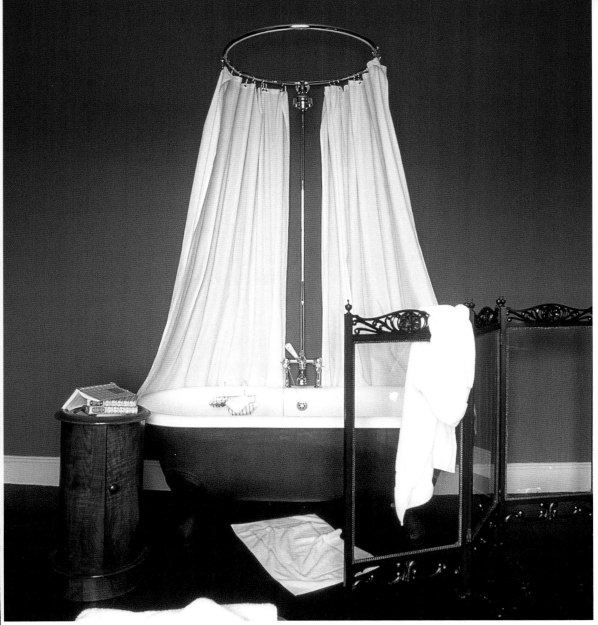

▲ A roll-top bath with a tall canopy is the focal point in this dramatic bathroom. Soft, sheer and light, the muslin hanging contrasts pleasantly.

ng beauties

e raw, hard,
finished textures
natural materials
uch as slate,
racotta, plaster
ceramic – can
en be the ideal
nplement to the
d tones of a
ple structural
hroom.

Bathroom textures

544

HONED SLATE
The interesting texture of
slate is highly suitable for a
classic-style bathroom.

482

PITTED PLASTER
A bare, distressed plaster
wall can make a striking
statement.

146

WOVEN FABRIC
A bathroom window
dressing need not be
too grand or complex.

582

ROUGH TERRACOTTA
Old and roughly pitted
terracotta has a fabulously
earthy, rustic texture.

99

SPONGED PAINTWORK
Sponging over a wet paint
colour gives a wall a three-
dimensional appearance.

448

CERAMIC TILES
Vivid tiling – here
with contrasting
grouting – adds
colour and texture.

swatch

(107)

▲ A hard wood floor and a soft wool rug: practical and comfortable in this home office, which has plenty of clever decorating id

Bright and businesslike

SURROUNDING YOURSELF WITH VIVID COLOUR WILL BRIGHTEN UP YO

WORKING ENVIRONMENT – BOTH LITERALLY AND EMOTIONALLY. LIFT YOUR SPIR

WITH BOLD PRIMARY SHADES AND A VARIETY OF FEEL-GOOD TEXTUR

bright and businesslike

Simple, attractive materials in a range of textures provide the solution for a smart and achievable home work room.

Home office textures

METAL MESH
Take a wastepaper basket made of metal mesh as a counterpoint to other, more solid, surfaces.

455

BAMBOO FLOORBOARDS
Amazingly tough and durable, bamboo makes a good choice for the floor of a home office.

506

LAMINATE SURFACE
Laminates – such as this lively embossed surface – can be used all over an office, from desktops to cupboard doors.

384

ACRYLIC SHEETING
Likewise, acrylics are ever-present in modern office furniture, and come in some glorious, intense colours.

361

CORK TILES
A cork noticeboard is one way to store memos and display mementoes, at the same time as providing another textural contrast.

305

WOOL CARPET
Don't forget home comforts like a toe-curlingly soft rug with deep woolen tufts.

262

Simple and inexpensive furniture that's both good-looking and practical is ideal when you're working from home, and a large desk, capacious storage and professional-quality chair are good places to start.

Here, a combination of white and apple green has been used for a cheerful, informal feel, teamed with touches of yellow, red and blue – it's certainly not your conventional, stuffy office. Note, too, how the textures vary in a pleasantly subtle way: the smooth hardness of the laminate desktop and storage units contrasts with the nubbly chair fabric, the soft pile of the rug, the opaque plastic of the computer casing and the wired-metal wastepaper basket. And, as a base to it all, the wooden floor has a gentle sheen and pretty pale colour that reflect the light and make the room more airy and inviting.

Intelligent innovations

There are some clever touches in this room that are worth emulating if you're thinking of setting up a home office of your own. The desk, for example, is curved for ease of working (with an attractive organic look) and has extending legs so you can adjust it to your height. The storage units dispense with unnecessary handles in favour of cut-out, circular finger-pulls, while the notice-board is simply a magnetised metal sheet. Finally, if you need to maximise every inch of your space (as most home offices do) consider wall-mounting your telephone, propping equipment on the tops of medium-height cabinets and buying a stool for your visitors to sit on – it simply tucks under the desk when not in use.

◀ Think through how much storage you'll need in advance, and plan what will go where; it will save time and effort in the long run.

▶ A slender chair with clean lines and a simple shape will help your office feel less cluttered.

Child's play

PLAYROOMS SHOULD BE FUN AND FUNCTIONAL,
[S]IMULATING YET SAFE. CREATE A FABULOUS CHILD'S
ROOM BY USING VIVID COLOURS COMBINED WITH
HARD-WEARING, EASY-TO-CLEAN MATERIALS.

[Th]e structural components of this room are neutral, while
[cu]shions, blinds and toys provide bright splashes of colour.

[Th]ese stackable cubes are an
[ma]tching method of storage.

▼ Wooden furniture is a tough and
good-looking choice for a child's room.

Children's toys almost inevitably come in bright colours,
which means you can design a playroom using fairly neutral
shades and still end up with a look that has enjoyable
impact. Wooden furniture is sturdy, inexpensive and easy to
care for; if, however, you (or your children) prefer a more
vivid scheme it can always be painted or stained. After
tables and chairs, storage is probably the biggest question in
designing this type of room: chests or boxes in wood or
plastic, preferably on casters for flexibility, are probably the
most practical, and can be as plain or as colourful as you
wish. For painting, drawing and homework, provide a solid,
spacious desk and a chair with good support.

Writing on the wall

On the walls, washable wallpaper in a subtle background
colour, inexpensive white emulsion (simply wash another
coat over if it gets dirty) and blackboard paint are all good
solutions. A playroom floor needs to be tough and durable,
but at the same time soft on the feet. Wooden boards with
comfortable (and sound-muffling) non-slip rugs, a carpet in
a colour that won't show the dirt, vinyl sheeting or maybe
even rubber would all be practical and good-looking.

Beanbags or large floor cushions are ideal for lounging
around, and will provide a cosy texture to contrast with
wood and plastic. Choose fabrics you can easily unzip and
throw into the washing machine, and bold shades that give
the whole look an attention-grabbing verve and vitality.

child's play

[T]he materials you pick for a child's bedroom or playroom need to
be hard-wearing, long-lasting and preferably washable. Within
these limits, however, there's plenty of scope for experimenting
with textures that will both look and feel great.

[C]hild-friendly textures

BOUCLE WOOL
[I]t's tough and won't show
dirt, but this fabric is also
enormously tactile.

128

WALLPAPER
This wallpaper looks just
like colourwashed wood,
but is much cheaper and
easier to install.

327

TOUGH COTTON
Thick cotton is ideal for a
[ch]air or beanbag cover, and
has a ribbed surface that
makes a pleasant change
from smoother canvas.

163

LINOLEUM
A grey lino with a small
pattern will hide the dirt;
it's inexpensive, soft
underfoot, and easy
to maintain.

339

▲ Beanbags are perfect for a child's playroom. Use a tactile
fabric for the cover, but make sure it's washable.

CHOOSE YOUR MATERIALS WITH CAR

FROM **PITTED** STONE T

SHINY GLASS, **SMOOT**

EMULSION TO **SOFT** SUEDE, EAC

HAS ITS OWN **QUALITIES** AN

USES – PLUS, OF COURSE,

UNIQUE TEXTURAL EFFEC

Practica
informatior

AINT

alls

tt emulsions are generally used for walls d ceilings. Water-based, they cover well, easily, and give a smooth, matt surface. a less standard finish, however, there is a alth of more specialist paints available, uding milk (casein) paints, soft

distemper/whitewash, limewash and various glazes and varnishes. Greater depth can be achieved with the application of special finishes such as dragging, sponging, rag-rolling or stippling.

Woodwork

The standard finish for woodwork is oil-based eggshell or gloss (although water-based varieties are also available), which are durable and easy to wipe clean. A special paint effect, such as graining, marbling or tortoiseshelling, adds interest.

Furniture

Flat oil paint is a good choice for painting furniture, protected, if necessary, with layers of clear varnish. Another good choice is eggshell or even matt emulsion, covered with matt varnish. Distressing, crackleglazing, marbling and gilding are among the many techniques available, either to disguise inferior wood or simply for decorative fun.

PAPERS

paint effects

A painted surface can provide a neutral background for other features in a room, or – if you use a paint effect – can add subtle interest in its own right. Traditional paint effects include dragging, combing and rag-rolling, while contemporary effects range from waxing and liming to crackling and splattering.

STIPPLING

STIPPLING

SPONGING

SPONGING

SPATTERING

RAGGING

RAGGING

COLOURWASHING

DRYBRUSHING

DRAGGING

DRAGGING

COMBING

CRACKLEUR

CRACKLEGLAZE

WAXING

LIMING

DISTRESSING

VERDE ANTICO

ANTIQUING

BRASS FINISH

Conventional wallpapers

Wallpaper offers character and is a good way to disguise less than perfect walls. The paper may be smooth or slightly three-dimensional featuring a raised or textured surface, and patterns can vary from small and intricate to modern versions with one, large graphic image per panel. Standard wallpapers will be spongeable (they can be wiped gently with soapy water), washable (they are covered with a thin plastic film and can be cleaned with water) or vinyl (they are covered with a tough plastic coating that means they can be scrubbed, making them a good choice for kitchens and bathrooms). It's a good idea to use inexpensive lining paper if your walls have imperfections that need disguising or prior to hanging heavy or expensive wallpapers; lining paper also provides a good base for painting. Always strip away old wallpaper before hanging new to provide a better base.

Unusual papers

Paper-backed surfaces such as grasscloth, thin cork, wood veneer, silk, woven raffia, metallic foil and hessian make an interesting

STRIPPING WALLPAPER

Hand-stripping standard wallpaper

1 Dampen old wallpaper with warm water, and sponge until the old paste is loosened and the paper is soft.

2 Scrape the paper off with a scraper, keeping it flat to wall to avoid gouging holes in plaster. Once the wall is smooth, allow it to dry before applying wallpaper or paint.

Machine-stripping wallpaper

1 Hire a steam stripper from your local tool shop. A stripper generates steam through the plate that is held against the wall, loosening the paper.

2 Scrape off the paper with a hand scraper.

Stripping paper-backed vinyl paper

1 Loosen a corner of paper and pull the top plastic layer back – upwards not outwards. The backing paper can be left as lining for the next wallcovering.

Stripping waterproof wallpaper

1 Use a sharp implement or serrated scraper to break through the surface.

2 Dampen the wallpaper with warm water. Strip paper as before.

HANGING WALLPAPER

1 Fill cracks and holes with filler. When dry, smooth with an abrasive paper.

2 Measure floor-to-ceiling height and add 10 cm (3 inches) to the total for trimming.

3 Use a plumb bob to ensure your first strip is hanging straight.

4 Measure and cut each piece of wallpaper and lay

right-side down on a clean work-table.

5 Mix the paste according to the packet's instructions. Brush the paste onto the paper, from the centre to the edge.

6 Fold paper with pasted area facing inwards and carry it to the wall.

7 Hang the paper, leaving enough overlap at the top for trimming.

8 Brush paper with hanging brush, using long, firm brushstrokes from centre of paper to edges.

9 Trim top and bottom of wallpaper.

10 Roll seams with boxwood roller, using sheet of paper to absorb excess paste.

---

statement, and can be hung in much the same way as ordinary wallpapers, either covering a whole wall or as a framed panel. Many types, however, are delicate and difficult to clean, and are thus better suited to low-traffic areas.

Floors

Flooring made from twisted paper yarn, sometimes mixed with sisal, is not nearly as fragile as you might imagine. In fact, it is surprisingly durable, and can be treated in the same way as natural fibre floorings.

TEXTILES

Curtains

Natural fibres – cotton, wool, silk and linen – are environmentally friendly, durable, tactile, and hang well. Inexpensive, simple and versatile, cotton comes in many different weights, from denim to muslin, and finishes, from velvet to chintz. Wool, from soft

cashmere to tough tweed, is flame-retardant and insulating. Silk, usually considered a luxury fabric, also comes in a wide range of weights and finishes; its soft, lustrous fibres make it a good insulator but less durable. Linen can range from crisp and sophisticated to crumpled and soft. It is extremely long-lasting and its matt surface means that it absorbs light.

Natural fibers need to be cleaned careful or else they may shrink or pucker. Synthetic fibres (the most common are acetate, polyester, acrylic and viscose) are water- an

STAIN REMOVAL

Always mop up or scrape off spills as soon as possible.

Removing greasy stains
1. Sprinkle an absorbent powder, such as talc, on the spill.
2. After half an hour, vacuum, shake or brush, then dry clean.

Colourfast linen
1. Stretch the fabric over a basin, sprinkle on powder detergent or stain remover.
2. Pour hot water through the fabric. Rinse. Rub stubborn stains with cleaner, rinse and wash.

Non-washable fabrics
1. Stretch the fabric over a basin, and pour cold water through the stain.
2. Work cleaning solution into stubborn stains, with an absorbent pad placed under the affected area.
3. Sponge with clear water and blot dry.

Emergency upholstery cleaner
1. Mix 1 part detergent to 4 parts boiling water. Cool to a jelly.
2. Whip with egg beater. Use the foam to clean upholstery.

STAIN	METHOD OF REMOVAL
Adhesives (clear and contact, latex, and model-maker's cement)	Apply acetone or non-oily nail varnish remover (except on acetates).
Adhesives (epoxy resin)	Do not allow the adhesive to dry. Apply methylated spirit to natural fabrics and lighter fuel to synthetics.
Adhesives (latex)	Remove with cold water before it dries. Peel off and dab remaining stain with grease solvent.
Adhesives (PVA or craft glue)	Apply methylated spirit.
Beer	Soak fresh stains with detergent or shampoo. For dried stains, use 1 egg cup of white vinegar to 600 ml (1 pint) of water. Blot from non-washables, dab with white vinegar and blot again.
Blood	Soak fresh stains in cold water. Soak up blood from non-washables with an absorbent pad, sponge with cold water containing drops of ammonia. Sponge a dried stain with salt water ($\frac{1}{2}$ tsp salt to 600 ml/1 pint water) or use biological detergent or carpet shampoo.
Candle wax	Chill with an ice cube, then scrape off with a blunt blade. Place slightly damp blotting or tissue paper over and under the wax. Press quickly with a warm iron until the wax is absorbed by the paper.
Chewing gum	Chill with an ice cube, scrape off, then use a dry cleaner.
Coffee/tea/chocolate	If dry, loosen the stain with glycerine. Use carpet shampoo or borax solution (mix one tbsp of borax in 600 ml/1 pint warm water).
Fruit juice	Apply borax solution or carpet shampoo. Sponge with a grease solvent on the wrong side of the fabric.
Ink (ballpoint)	Rinse in cold water, then wash. Dab non-washables with nail varnish remover (except on acetates).
Ink (felt-tip)	Apply methylated spirit.
Lemon juice	Apply borax solution, then wash.
Mildew	Brush off excess, then use carpet shampoo.
Milk	Rinse fresh stains in lukewarm water. Use borax solution or carpet shampoo on dried stains.
Paint (oil and enamel)	Apply paint remover or turpentine.
Paint (fresh emulsion)	Rinse with cold water.
Soft drinks	Rinse with boiling water, then wash.
Wine	Add 1 egg cup of white vinegar to 600 ml/1 pint of water, or use a biological detergent or shampoo solution.
Wine (white)	Rinse with warm water. If necessary, sponge with borax solution.
Wine (red)	If washable, sponge with white wine, then rinse with warm water. If necessary, sponge with borax solution. Or cover with salt to absorb the wine then stretch the material over a basin and pour through boiling water. If non-washable, use upholstery shampoo or sponge with warm water, blot. Sprinkle on talc, leave for an hour. Sponge and blot again

stain-resistant, strong and long-lasting; often the most satisfactory fabrics for curtains are made from a blend of man-made and natural fibres. Vacuum curtains gently every month and clean thoroughly every few years; some types can be washed (always follow the manufacturer's advice carefully), others must be dry cleaned. Linings may need to be removed to avoid shrinking at different rates.

Upholstery

Use upholstery-weight fabric that has been rub-tested by the manufacturer. It should also be flame-retardant and, ideally, have been given a stain-resistant treatment. Loose-weave or textured fabrics will snag more easily than smooth, tightly woven fabrics.

SKINS AND FAKE FUR

Leather

Upholstery should be dusted regularly, and occasionally given hide food to prevent it from drying out and to prevent stains. Keep away from direct heat, which may cause cracking. Clean by wiping with a soft, damp cloth. However, some leathers should not be wetted – check the manufacturer's instructions. Leather floors are available in irregularly shaped sheets and tiles. Warm, soft, and quiet underfoot, they need to be waxed regularly and are then relatively easy to keep clean, although they do stain and scratch easily. If treated well, they can last a lifetime, aging naturally like a favourite pair of shoes.

Suede

Suede can be protected with a spray (test first on a hidden area). Wipe dirty suede with a clean, damp cloth and allow to dry naturally. Brush with a suede block. For serious soiling have it professionally cleaned. Alcantara is a cheaper, suede-effect man-made fabric that can be used in the same way. Nubuck, made from cow leather, looks similar to suede; do not, however, use suede shampoos or brushes on it as they may damage the pile. Use a specialist nubuck or calf-leather cleaner instead.

Fake fur

Fake fur is as attractive and tactile as real fur. It should always be dry cleaned. Clean light soiling by sponging with a warm solution of non-biological washing powder and shaking well before allowing to dry naturally.

CARPET

Carpet is warm and soft underfoot and has good soundproofing and insulating qualities. Its durability and resistance to wear is determined by pile height and density. In general, halls and stairs need heavy-duty carpets, living and dining rooms medium-duty, and bedrooms can be lightweight. Carpets are not usually recommended for bathrooms, kitchens, utility rooms or conservatories, although some versions are water-resistant.

There are two basic types of carpet construction: woven (very hard-wearing and more expensive) and tufted. Pile types include loop, twist, velvet, cord, shag, saxony, and cut and loop – each gives a different effect and some are more suitable for certain areas than others: shag pile, for example, is dangerous on stairs.

Carpets can be made from a variety of

materials. Of the natural fibres, wool is hard-wearing, relatively easy to clean and fire-retardant; linen, cotton and silk are wonderfully luxurious, but more decorative than durable. Man-made fibres are less expensive and are often blended with wool to combine their best qualities. A mix of 80 percent wool and 20 percent nylon, for example, is often cited as desirable.

To make your carpet last longer, buy one that has received a stain-resistant/retardant treatment during manufacture and use a high-quality underlay (unless the carpet has its own foam backing). Never use old underlay with a new carpet. Place caster cups under the feet of heavy furniture to minimise denting. Vacuuming a carpet regularly keeps the pile vertical and thus reduces shading, and prevents grit becoming embedded and wearing the fibres away. Mop up spills quickly, rubbing gently from the edge inward. An occasional dry or wet shampoo is usually a good idea – check the care instructions supplied with the carpet. Brand-name stain removers are available; professional cleaning is, however, advisable for stubborn stains.

NATURAL FIBRE FLOORINGS

Woven or plaited sisal, coir, seagrass, rush and jute have been used as floorings for centuries; today they are available in a wide range of colours and patterns, are warm, soundproof and insulating, and frequently offer good value for money. Coir and sisal, especially, are extremely tough and hard-wearing, though some may find their

carpet

The variety in construction styles means you can match the carpet's pile to its environment.

LOOPED PILE   TWISTED PILE

CORD PILE   CUT PILE

VELVET PILE   SHAG PILE

rough surface uncomfortable underfoot. F[or] the softest feel in a fibre flooring, opt for j[ute] (though it's the least hard-wearing). Like carpet, natural floorings are not always practical in kitchens or bathrooms, and yo[u] should be careful using them on stairs. Ru[sh] and jute are not really suitable, while seag[rass] must be laid with the warp parallel with th[e] stair tread to ensure a good grip. Always consult your retailer for advice on the suitability of a particular fibre flooring for it[s] intended use.

Natural fibre flooring doesn't show dirt badly, but it does need to be vacuumed regularly with a suction (not brush) cleane[r]. If the covering is not latex-backed, lift it an[d] vacuum the floor underneath, too. Backing and underlay is advisable for fitted flooring, however, for comfort, wear and insulation. And it's a good idea to buy floorings that have already been treated with a stain inhibitor, as stains can be hard to remove. To clean dirt or mud, allow to dry then loos[en] with a stiff brush before vacuuming. Spills should be blotted promptly with absorbent

er or a sponge and wiped over with a
mp cloth. Dry-cleaning shampoo may get
of stains. Don't soak sisal, coir or jute
h water or use wet shampoo. Rush, on
other hand, will crumble if it becomes
dry, so it occasionally needs a light
aying of water.

RICK

oors

ring made of high-fired paving bricks
vers) is most suitable for hallways, rustic
hens, dining areas and conservatories,
g non-slip, tough and rugged in
earance. New or reclaimed bricks come
oft, varied colours and can be laid in a
ety of patterns. Though hard and slightly
gh underfoot, they're warmer than marble
eramic tiles. Like any hard surface,
ever, they will not be kind to dropped
ckery. Stains can be hard to remove from
kwork; to avoid staining, bricks may be
ed with boiled linseed oil or polyurethane
ish thinned with white spirit, but it will
their surface character. Generally, clean
weeping or use a stiff brush and plain
water. Always ask your supplier for advice
naintenance.

erior walls

or walls made of good-condition brick
be left bare, giving an attractively rustic
. To prevent them from shedding fine
cles of sand, and to make them easier to
, seal the walls with PVA adhesive
ned 1:5 with water (this will enrich the
ur slightly). Alternatively, apply paint
ght onto the walls.

CANE

Furniture

Though light and strong, bamboo and rattan
furniture can split quite easily, and is then
almost impossible to mend – but it will last a
long time if well cared for. Clean by wiping
with water or a solution of washing-up liquid,
but do not over-wet. Do not leave outdoors.
If cane furniture does become soaked, allow
to dry naturally, away from direct heat.

Floors

Floorboards made from lacquered bamboo
are tough, durable and extremely
environmentally friendly. They can be
treated like a hardwood floor, with the
difference that they're also suitable for
use in humid rooms such as bathrooms
or conservatories.

CERAMIC TILES

Walls

Ceramic wall tiles are hard-wearing, low-
maintenance and hygienic, and thus highly
suitable for hallways, and splashbacks in
kitchens and bathrooms. You can lay new
tiles directly over old ones, providing the
surface is even, or else paint over them. First,
wash thoroughly with sugar soap or a
detergent solution, then coat with primer
followed by a solvent-based paint. To clean,
wipe with an all-purpose anti-bacterial cleaner,
avoiding abrasives.

Floors

Thicker than wall tiles, ceramic floor tiles are
heat- and water-resistant, hard-wearing and
low-maintenance, but may be noisy and
tiring on the feet, and are liable to crack if
something hard is dropped on them. Use with
underfloor heating for warmth. Ideal for
bathrooms, kitchens, halls and conservatories
(use frostproof tiles in the latter). Glazed
ceramic tiles are slippery when wet: use
unglazed (quarry or terracotta), textured or
matt tiles for grip. Terracotta tiles can be
sealed with a recommended sealant or with
linseed oil and floor wax, which darkens their
colour slightly. Don't seal or polish non-porous
ceramic tiles – the product won't be absorbed,
and the tiles will become slippery and attract
dirt. Clean ceramic tiles by sweeping, then
mopping with a mild detergent. Buff with a
soft cloth but don't polish. Harsh abrasives
can damage glazed tiles.

Worktops

Tiled kitchen worktops must be laid evenly
and flat, and cleaned carefully, as the grout
can harbor germs. The tiles are liable to craze
and crack if not treated with some care,

ceramic

CLEANING CERAMIC TILES

1 Sweep tiles, then mop with mild
detergent, not harsh abrasives.

2 Clean dirty grout with an old toothbrush
dipped in 1 part bleach to 4 parts water.
Then rinse.

3 Buff tiles with a soft cloth – don't polish.

step by step

though individual tiles can be replaced. If grout becomes dirty, use an old toothbrush dipped in one part bleach to four parts water, scrub carefully, then rinse.

CONCRETE

Worktops

Durable and long-lasting, worktops made from reinforced concrete can be custom-moulded and coloured, with a matt or smooth finish. Seal before use with several applications of an alcohol-based sealant, and finish with wax – this needs to be reapplied occasionally. Clean with a mild, non-abrasive cleaner, such as soap and water.

Floors

Poured concrete floors can be affordable and surprisingly versatile – and are not necessarily for use just in kitchens and conservatories. Though cold and hard underfoot, they are extremely durable and heat- and scratch-resistant. Left bare, they have a raw, ascetic quality. Less austere finishes include hammering, scoring, sandblasting, painting, staining, veining, polishing (with several coats of wax followed by machine buffing) and imprinting with patterns. Concrete paving can be used exactly like stone slabs. Seal before use to avoid staining – ask your supplier to recommend a suitable sealant.

GLASS

Windows and doors

Alternatives to clear glass include sand-blasted, acid-etched, stained, textured and patterned – not to mention hi-tech types such as the version that turns from clear to opaque when touched. French windows and large, low panes should be made of toughened or laminated glass, or covered with a special safety film: if broken, they won't shatter into hundreds of dangerously sharp pieces.

As an alternative to chemical window cleaners, use a mix of 30 ml (2 tbsp) of vinegar or methylated spirits mixed with 4 litres (9 pints) of water. Apply mixture with a lint-free cloth, and buff the window with scrunched-up newspaper.

Splashbacks

Waterproof, heat-resistant (except under extreme temperatures), and easy to clean, a thick sheet of laminated glass makes a beautiful splashback, though it will scratch or break if struck by a hard object. Lights fitted behind or above make an even bigger impact.

Floors

A glass sheet or block floor (or staircase) makes an impressive statement, though it must be installed by a specialist. It can be very slippery, however, and requires frequent cleaning; opaque glass is a better choice than clear, as scratches won't be so noticeable.

LAMINATES

Work surfaces

Made from a chipboard base topped by a thin sheet of laminate, these inexpensive and low-maintenance surfaces are usually used in kitchens and bathrooms (and sometimes on walls, too). They come in an enormous variety of colours, textures and patterns, many of them good imitations of stone, wood and other natural materials, though the surface does, inevitably, feel different. Edges can be square or rounded (post-formed); the latter is less likely to ch Cheaper versions are sometimes not especially heat- or knife-resistant – high-pressure laminates are a better choice for long-lasting kitchen worktops. Ensure that the underside is sealed, to prevent water damage from appliances placed underneat To clean, wipe with an all-purpose anti-bacterial cleaner. Stains can be removed with a slightly abrasive cream cleaner, diluted bleach or even a solvent such as methylated spirits, white spirit, or nail varnish remover (check with the manufacturer first). Chips in laminated surfaces can usually be filled with a purpos made laminate repairer applied in several thin layers.

REPAINTING PAINTED METAL AND WROUGHT-IRON FURNITURE

1 Annually, remove rust with wire wool.

2 Apply anti-rust primer immediately.

3 Apply a coat of exterior metal paint.

4 If furniture is cast-aluminium, wipe with a solution of detergent and paint over any chips with metal paint.

...n-made solid surfaces

...e with a combination of minerals and ...lic resin, these composite surfaces are ...-porous, stain-resistant, easy to clean, and ...e in a wide range of colours and patterns. ...y can be manufactured to any seamless ...e, but they must be professionally ...alled. They are heat- and stain-resistant, ...it is possible for slight burns or scratches ...e sanded out (severe damage should be ...aired by the manufacturer). Wipe with an ...urpose, anti-bacterial cleaner. Abrasive ...m cleaners can be used on stained ...aces, as can solvents, though the latter ...uld always be thoroughly rinsed away.

...ETAL

the kitchen

...et-metal work surfaces, sinks and ...shbacks are hygienic, heat-proof and very durable, but tend to scratch, show fingermarks and eventually assume a natural, worn-in patina. Brushed stainless steel is expensive but usually regarded as the most desirable; galvanised steel looks more industrial but is cheaper. Clean frequently with a non-abrasive liquid or cream; stainless steel can be treated occasionally with baby oil for protection. Bleaching may cause corrosion. Zinc and anodised aluminium are best used for splashbacks only; the former marks easily and dulls over time, resulting in a characterful appearance, while the latter is non-corrosive and light, but dents easily and will eventually become soft and dull.

Garden furniture

Repaint cast- and wrought-iron chairs and tables annually – after first rubbing down with wire wool – using anti-rust primer and exterior metal paint. Cast-aluminium furniture doesn't rust; simply wipe with a solution of washing-up liquid, and touch up chips with metal paint.

Floors

Sheet- or tiled-metal floors (made of stainless or galvanised steel, aluminium, copper or zinc) are highly tough and resilient, though they do eventually wear to a pleasant patina. Finishes vary from brushed or polished to oxidised or pressed with a diamond pattern for better grip. Sheets of metal should be welded to a level timber base in order to minimise tinny noise. Ask your supplier for advice on sealing and cleaning.

Door knobs

Door furniture (knobs, handles and fingerplates) is usually lacquered by the manufacturer, and so simply needs dusting and occasional washing in a soapy solution. Avoid abrasive cleaners that can damage the surface.

PLASTER

Plaster walls and ceilings are traditionally covered with wallpaper, paint, tiles or some other form of surface. But don't rule out bare plaster, which can be surprisingly attractive, as well as relatively durable and inexpensive. You could choose the more usual finishes such as the standard buff pink, white (with the addition of kaolin), textured (with the application of, perhaps, straw, sand, or sawdust), combed into patterns, sparkled (by working in marble or metallic dust), polished or stained. Plaster doesn't take kindly to water, however. Make sure that you install a splashback to protect bare plaster walls in the kitchen or bathroom. Unusual plaster and plaster-like finishes, such as stucco, gesso, fresco, scagliola and marmorino, also create impressive effects.

SHEET FLOORINGS

Though not especially luxurious, these floorings are quiet, soft and warm underfoot, strong, flexible, low-maintenance and easy to clean. They're relatively inexpensive and easy to install, and computer-controlled cutting allows an extensive variety of patterns. These floorings are also available as tiles.

Vinyl

A PVC-based man-made material, vinyl comes in a variety of textures, patterns, colours and thicknesses. Thin vinyls can be cold and hard;

thicker vinyl is more expensive but also more cushioning, durable and insulating. Some types are excellent imitations of wood or stone flooring. Vinyl is waterproof and stain-resistant, but may burn, scratch and dent. If constantly soaked, it may lift up, and less expensive vinyls may discolour with age. Vacuum or sweep regularly to keep clear of grit, which will damage its surface. Wash with a mild washing-up liquid solution or a recommended cleaner, and rinse thoroughly. Avoid harsh abrasives and polishes; the former may mar the surface, the latter may make it slippery. The manufacturer's recommended floor dressing should help reduce staining.

Linoleum

Linoleum – or lino – is made from linseed oil, ground cork, wood flour and resins, pressed onto a jute or hessian backing. It's resistant to stains, abrasions and burns, as well as being non-slip, and available in a huge range of colours and patterns. For extra cushioning or sound insulation, or where the sub-floor is particularly uneven, you can buy lino that is backed with cork. Clean regularly by sweeping and washing with a mild detergent solution and, if you wish, applying a water-based emulsion polish. Don't wax polish lino, though, and avoid strong alkaline cleaning agents. Instead, revive worn lino with a special linoleum paint. And avoid allowing water to get underneath it, too, as this will cause it to lift.

Cork

Environmentally friendly cork is lightweight yet hard-wearing, cushioning and excellent for insulation, though it will lift if laid on a damp floor or over underfloor heating. Cork floors should usually be sealed with a polyurethane varnish. They can be sanded down (and resealed) if worn. Mop with a

vinyl

REPLACING VINYL TILES

1 Heat the damaged tile with a hot iron to soften the adhesive. Lift a corner of the old tile with a filling knife and peel off the tile.

2 Remove the old adhesive with a scraper and clean the area. Trim a new tile to fit.

3 Evenly apply vinyl-tile adhesive to the area with an adhesive spreader.

4 Warm a new tile with an iron. Once placed, lay a board over the tile and weigh it down until the adhesive sets.

washing-up liquid solution and, if you wish, emulsion-polish occasionally to give added protection.

Rubber

Flexible, waterproof and tough, rubber can be coloured, patterned, smooth or studded and is often considered a good option for a bathroom or hallway (smooth versions, however, may be slippery when wet – consult your retailer for advice). Rubber can be left matt or polished; the latter intensifies color and makes it less liable to mark and stain. Dirt tends to gather on textured surfaces, and watch out for hot items, which may burn the rubber. Sweep and mop clean with a mild detergent. A natural bristle brush (or even an old toothbrush!) can loosen dirt in pattern treads.

STONE

Stone is unbeatably elegant, comes in a variety of subtle natural tones and will last a lifetime (or more) with little maintenance. However, it is also expensive and generally considered cold, noisy, and hard on the feet.

Floors

There are three categories of stone. The 'softest' are sandstone and limestone, whic can be given a honed (smooth and matt) c sanded (rougher) finish, and contain obvic flecks, fossils and sediment formations. Because they're porous they need to be sealed to prevent staining; the best metho by silicone impregnation, which hardly changes the surface and allows the stone t age naturally. Sweep and wash regularly w a mild soap.

Slate is a harder stone, almost as durab as marble and granite, and can be finished various textures: riven (unevenly hand-spl flame-textured (machine-cut with the surfa roughened by a flame), sanded (flat but nc polished), honed (smooth and matt), and polished. To prevent oil stains, slate may b sealed with a recommended sealer. It can b cleaned by buffing with a nylon pad; neutr detergent may get rid of stains.

Marble, which can be highly polished c left matt, is extremely dense and can be precision-cut; it's impervious to water and therefore, a good choice for bathrooms, though it can be slippery when wet. It's best avoided in a kitchen, however, as it ca be stained and corroded by acidic solution It requires hardly any cleaning other than a rub with a chamois leather dipped in clean water.

anite is the most durable of all building
s. It's very suitable for kitchens, though
ed versions are highly slippery when
o it may be better to choose a honed or
d version. Clean with water and never
floor polish, as this will attract dirt.
ally, terrazzo is an equally durable but
xpensive marble/granite substitute,
of a mix of marble chippings in a
t base, formed into tiles or laid wet
y onto the floor.

rktops

ed or honed granite, slate and terrazzo
surfaces look attractive and are heat-
hard-wearing and impervious to
(slate must be sealed to reduce
ty), but are expensive and tricky to
Use limestone and marble with
n: both can scratch and stain easily;
nust be treated with a solvent-based
sealant. Clean stone worktops by
g with a mild anti-bacterial cleaner and
thoroughly with a soft cloth. Avoid
or abrasive cleaners.

WOOD

Floors

Although not as cosy underfoot as carpet,
wooden floors are good-looking, available in
a variety of styles, and don't harbour dust.
Because they can sometimes warp, they are
not suitable for conservatories or very wet or
steamy bathrooms.

Solid wood floors are usually made of a
hardwood such as oak, beech, ash, maple or
mahogany, and come in boards or blocks in a
range of thicknesses (the thicker the wood,
the longer it will last but the more it will
cost). When buying new hardwood, ensure
that it comes from an environmentally
friendly source. Alternatively, recycled wood
can be extremely attractive. Softwoods,
such as pine or spruce, wear more quickly;
hardwood floors, however, can last a lifetime.

Less expensive is a multi-layered or
veneered wood floor, where a thin hardwood
surface covers a base of cheaper wood, MDF,
cork or plywood. These can be more sound-
absorbent than solid wood floors, but won't
last as long.

Wood floors should nearly always be
sealed. Waxed floors need regular polishing
and re-waxing – and beware slippery rugs
(special underlay reduces this problem). Oiled
wood floors have a mellow sheen; similarly,
they need regular re-oiling. Varnish or lacquer,
in matt or gloss, is highly durable, especially if
painted on in many thin layers, and sanded
between each application. Floor paints or
stains can be used to disguise inferior wood.

Wooden floors can be damaged by
cigarettes, high heels and furniture; to avoid
the latter, place protective pads under
furniture. Damage to a solid wood floor can,
however, be sanded out. Clean wooden floors
by regular sweeping or vacuuming, and
wiping with a damp mop. Spills should be
mopped up immediately.

Kitchen worktops

Solid wood work surfaces are relatively heat-
resistant, and minor burns or knife marks can
simply be sanded out. They do, however,
need to be well-sealed for both hygiene and
durability. A coating of varnish, linseed oil or
beeswax will do the trick; all need regular top-
ups. When cleaning, avoid harsh detergents,
and dry thoroughly afterward.

Furniture

Lacquered-wood furniture doesn't need
polishing; just wipe it with a damp duster.
Grease can be removed with a mild solution
of soap flakes. For unsealed (waxed or French
polished) wooden furniture, simply dust with
a dry cloth and apply a wax polish once or
twice a year. Remove sticky marks in the same
way as above, drying the wood carefully with
a soft cloth afterward.

wood

SANDING FLOORBOARDS

Hire an industrial sanding machine from your local tool outlet for main floor area and a
smaller hand disc sander for edges. Clear the room of furniture, curtains and pictures.
Close and seal doors with masking tape. Open windows. Remember to wear face mask.

Before switching
n a sanding
machine, tilt it back
o lift it off the floor.
witch on and slowly
ower onto floor.

2 Sand parallel to the
floorboards, never
across. Move the
machine forwards and
backwards, but keep
it moving to avoid
making a groove in
the floorboards.

3 Sand the edges of
the room with a
smaller rotary sander.
Again, tilt the sander
back before
switching on and
lower gently onto
floor.

4 Finish the areas
closest to the wall
and corners with a
scraper. Vacuum the
floor and wipe with a
cloth dampened with
white spirit.

Index

a

accessories 6, 19, 20, 24, 25, 32, 33, 41, 42, 44, 45, 56, 58, 59, 60, 64, 65, 76, 79, 84, 85, 86, 87, 103

b

bamboo: furniture 42
　　　　mat 22, 23
baskets 20, 31, 60, 61, 70, 71, 72, 76
bathroom 40–1, 42–3, 44–5, 72–3, 74–5, 104–5, 106–7
beanbag 111
bedroom 26–7, 28–9, 30–1, 60–1, 62–3, 64–5, 90–1, 92–3, 94–5
brick 33, 61, 117

c

cane 23, 117
carpet 55, 56, 60, 61, 65, 71, 85, 111, 116
　　pile 116
ceiling 86, 101
ceramic tiles 44, 117–18
　　cleaning 117
　　on floors 41
　　on walls 38, 40, 41, 68, 69, 72, 72, 106
child's room 110–11
concrete 58, 86, 118
cork 24, 120
curtains 10, 19, 24, 25, 65, 85, 86, 88, 96
　　bed 60, 62

cushions 21, 24, 25, 28, 31, 5 56, 57, 61, 65, 88, 96
　　floor 28, 85, 111

d

dining room 36–7, 70–1, 102

f

fake fur 21, 29, 54, 62, 116
floors 10, 114, 116–17, 118, 119–21
　　concrete 86, 118
　　leather 115
　　linoleum 71, 120
　　metal 67
　　natural fibres 21, 27, 49, 5 61, 65, 71, 86, 94, 116
　　paper 7, 114
　　pebble 36
　　rubber 71
　　stone 23, 41, 67, 75, 86, 101 106, 120
　　terrazzo 39
　　wood 23, 28, 36, 42, 55, 61, 71, 75, 89, 90, 96, 99, 106,
　　tiled 41
　　see also carpets, linoleum, ru
furniture: glass 54, 101
　　leather 24, 58
　　metal 39, 90
　　plastic 36, 39, 79, 101, 103
　　rattan 24
　　upholstered 23, 24, 28, 31, 62, 76, 89, 101
　　wood 21, 24, 27, 36, 49, 54 62, 65, 68, 71, 86, 96, 101,

79, 99, 100, 105, 118
bathroom 40, 41
niture 54, 100, 101

e office 46–7, 48–9, 76–7,
–9, 108–9

en 32–3, 34–5, 38–9, 66–7,
–9, 98–9, 100–1

hates 10, 72, 109, 118–19
her 115
niture 6, 19, 24, 25, 58, 59
ing 12, 18, 19, 24, 47, 48,
, 55, 60, 65, 79, 89, 90, 96,

eum 71, 120
g room 18–19, 20–1, 22–3,
–5, 54–5, 56–7, 58–9, 84–5,
–7, 88–9

ole 39, 44, 45, 75, 106
al 118, 119
bathrooms 41
oring 53, 67
rniture 28, 39, 90, 91,
6

in kitchens 38, 39, 66, 67,
101
painted 118
metallic paint 75
mirrors 28, 42, 44, 62, 74, 75,
105
mosaic tiles 41, 105, 106

n
natural fibres 114
flooring 21, 27, 48, 49, 55, 61,
65, 71, 86, 94, 116

p
paint: effects 106, 113
types 113
paper flooring 114
plaster walls 42, 43, 61, 72, 86,
90
plastic furniture 36, 39, 79, 89,
101, 102, 103

q
quarry tiles 33

r
rattan furniture 23, 24, 25, 57
replacing vinyl tiles 120
rubber 105, 120
flooring 71
rugs 10, 11, 19, 23, 24, 27, 49,
55, 58, 64, 85, 89, 108, 111

s
sanding floors 121
slate 106
stain removal 115
stripping wallpaper 114
stone: flooring 23, 41, 67, 75,
86, 101, 106, 120
worktop 67, 101
storage 31, 33, 34, 36, 47, 47,
65, 67, 68, 72, 76, 79, 96, 99,
105, 109, 111
suede 25, 115–16

t
teenager's room 96–7
terrazzo flooring 39
textiles 19, 24, 28, 31, 85, 103
bedroom 27, 28, 60, 62, 63,
65, 90, 91, 94, 96
upholstery 18, 19, 23, 24, 28,
55, 56, 62, 86, 89, 101
throws 10, 24, 28, 31, 54, 55, 56,
61, 62, 64, 90, 96
tiles: ceramic 38, 41, 44, 68, 72,
106, 117–18
marble 44
mosaic 41, 105, 106
quarry 33
slate 106
vinyl 120
trimmings 24, 27, 55, 61, 85

u
upholstered furniture 23, 24, 28,
30, 31, 55, 62, 76, 86, 89, 101

v
vinyl 75, 119–20
replacing tiles 120

w
wall coverings 24, 72, 86, 106
*see also wallpaper, walls, wood
paneling*
wallpaper 24, 111, 113–14
stripping 114
walls 10, 24, 72, 86, 106, 111,
113–14
cork 24
plaster 42, 61, 72, 86, 90
wood 23, 27, 42, 49, 61, 67,
72, 106
wicker 11, 31, 39, 60, 61, 70, 71,
72
windows 19, 24, 86, 118
cleaning 118
wood: care of 121
in kitchens 68, 98
wood paneling 23, 26, 27, 42,
49, 61, 67, 72, 106
wooden floors 23, 29, 42, 43, 54,
55, 61, 65, 71, 89, 90, 96, 99,
106, 108, 111, 121
limewashed 28, 36, 71, 75
sanding 121
wooden furniture 21, 24, 27, 36,
39, 49, 49, 54, 62, 65, 68, 71,
86, 96, 101, 111